CHINA MIRACLE

CHINA MIRACLE

A Voice to the Church in the West

ARTHUR WALLIS

KINGSWAY PUBLICATIONS
EASTBOURNE

ISBN 0 86065 415 X

Printed in Great Britain for
KINGSWAY PUBLICATIONS LTD
Lottbridge Drove, Eastbourne, E. Sussex BN23 6NT by
Richard Clay (The Chaucer Press) Ltd, Bungay, Suffolk
Typeset by Nuprint Services Ltd, Harpenden, Herts AL5 4SE

THE CHURCH IN CHINA

'Hard pressed on every side, but not crushed; perplexed, but not in despair; persecuted, but not abandoned; struck down, but not destroyed'—across the divide men call 'the Bamboo Curtain' you speak to us in the ease and comfort of the West. With all your deprivations and restrictions, you demonstrate to us something of the rugged grandeur of New Testament Christianity, that we, with all our privileges, so sadly lack—

to you this book is affectionately dedicated.

CONTENTS

THANK YOU

To Paul Kauffman whose book, *China, the Emerging Challenge*, was my early inspiration, and who was such an encouragement to me when we met in Hong Kong.

To others whose books have greatly helped me, especially Leslie Lyall's *God Reigns in China*, David Adeney's *Christian Students Face the Revolution* and Carl Lawrence's *The Church in China*. Where I have been granted permission to quote from these and other writings, this has been acknowledged in the footnotes.

To various China Ministries in Hong Kong, especially the Chinese Church Research Centre, Christian Communications, Asian Outreach and Open Doors, whose communications have given me up to date information about the church on the mainland.

To David Wang for his help and encouragement, and especially for the transcript of a message on what God is saying to us through the Church in China.

To Ross Paterson who generously put his China material at my disposal and put me in touch with Tony Lambert. To them both for reading my script with great care and putting me right on a number of details.

To Susan Rackstraw of OMF for supplying photos.

To Alan Boardman for the map of China.

To Rick Bradley for the drawing of Pastor Hsi.

To Diana Moss, for all her typing and re-typing.

Last, but by no means least, to my wife and partner in the work, Eileen, who has been a constant source of help and encouragement.

IMPORTANT DATES

1766–1122 B.C.	The Shang dynasty flourished in the Yellow River valley. This was about the time of Moses.
255–206 B.C.	The Qin (Ch'in) dynasty that gave China its name, produced its first emperor who unified the languages, constructed the Great Wall, and brought much reform.
1644–1911 A.D.	The Qing (Ch'ing or Manchu) dynasty. The Manchus came from the North. Abdication of the last Manchu emperor in 1911 ended 3,600 years of dynastic rule in China.
1807	Robert Morrison, first Protestant missionary to China, arrived in Macau.
1822	First modern-day version of the Bible in Chinese.
1839–1842	The First Opium War, Britain versus China.
1856–1860	The Second Opium War, Britain and France versus China.
1900	Boxer Rebellion. 186 Protestant missionaries martyred.
1912	Sun Yat-sen inaugurated as the first president of the Republic of China. Ousted six weeks later.
1919	Versailles Treaty of World War 1 that handed Chinese territory to Japan.

1922	Sun Yat-sen restored to power.
1934–1936	The Long March, strategic retreat of the Communist Armies from the Nationalist (Kuomintang) Armies.
1937–1945	The Sino-Japanese War.
1945–1949	Civil War between the Nationalists and the Communists.
1949–October	Proclamation in Beijing (Peking) of The People's Republic of China by Mao Zedong, its first chairman. The Nationalists set up their base in Taiwan.
1951–1952	Land Reform Campaign. Private land confiscated. Campaigns against Capitalists.
1952	All missionaries finally driven out of China.
1954	Three-Self Patriotic Movement constituted.
1956	The Hundred Flowers Movement.
1958	All Christian denominations finally dissolved.
1958	The Great Leap Forward.
1966–1976	The Great Cultural Revolution.
1971	China admitted to the United Nations.
1976	Deaths of Premier Zhou-Enlai and of Chairman Mao Zedong. Arrest of the Gang of Four.
1978	Emergence of Deng Xiaoping as No. 1 in China. The Four Modernizations Programme aimed at agriculture, industry, defence and science.

Map of
THE PEOPLE'S REPUBLIC
OF CHINA

PART ONE

China Tells Her Story

Chapter One

WHY 'CHINA MIRACLE'?

*Who among the gods is like you, O Lord? Who is
like you—majestic in holiness, awesome in glory,
working wonders?*

Exodus 15:11

Many believers are aware that there has recently been
some kind of revival of Christianity in China. But how
extensive is it? Is there really any justification for describing it as 'a miracle'? Let us answer that by considering for a moment the circumstances in which God has
been working.

On my first visit to China I was agreeably surprised
at the freedom that there appeared to be. It seemed I
could go anywhere and speak to anyone without restric-
tion. 'I've never been to Russia,' I remarked to a leading
correspondent in Beijing (Peking), 'but I would imagine
there is much more freedom here in China.' He shook
his head and smiled. 'You don't understand how the
system works. It is not you they are watching so much
as the Chinese people who talk to you. They could well
be required, after you have gone, to explain their contact
with a foreigner.'

I soon discovered that there was a nation-wide spy

system. As a Chinese citizen, any suspicious action where you live could be reported to your street committee. Any irregularities at your work-place could be reported to your 'danwei' or work committee. There they would have a complete dossier on you. In theory, everybody spies on everybody else. You are not free to get engaged, marry, move house, change job etc., without reference to your danwei. The People's Republic is changing, but it has been one of the most repressive and restrictive regimes in the world. It is in this political context that God has been at work.

On top of all that, the darkest period of the church in China during the thirty-five years of Communist rule was 'The Great Cultural Revolution'. Churches were compulsorily closed, pastors imprisoned and bonfires made of Bibles and Christian books. It seemed to outside observers that the church in China had been wiped out. For God to revive his church in the normal political context of Communist China would have been remarkable, but to resurrect his church out of the ashes of the Cultural Revolution, must be regarded as nothing short of a miracle.

Geographically, China is one of the largest countries in the world. This movement of the Holy Spirit has not been confined to a few bright spots, nor even to the areas where missionaries formerly laboured. It has reached almost all of China's twenty-nine provinces, autonomous regions and municipalities—from the desolate Steppes of Inner Mongolia in the North to the mountain tribes of the South-West; and from the coastal provinces with their teeming millions, to the mountainous borders of Tibet. The incredible range of this movement qualifies it to be called a miracle.

Furthermore, China is numerically the greatest nation, with its 'one billion plus' population. One out of every four human beings is Chinese. When the Communists came to power in 1949 there were approximately four million Catholics and one million Protestants in China, but this figure was drastically reduced during the Cultural Revolution. By 1983 it was estimated that there were probably fifty million Bible-believing Christians, or 5% of the population.

When you consider that this phenomenal multiplication occurred when so many pastors and mature leaders were in prison, and when Bibles and Christian literature were in grievously short supply, that must surely be, by any standards, a miracle. The movement has been described as 'the most rapid church growth in the history of Christianity'. Others have pointed out that the church in China now represents the largest body of believers in the world.

As a young Christian I had read most of the great missionary biographies dealing with China—Hudson Taylor, the Cambridge Seven, the *Triumph of John and Betty Stam*, as well as those of the great Chinese leaders, Pastor Hsi, John Sung and most notably the teachings of Watchman Nee. 'The magic and mystique of China' fascinated and frightened me. 'It must be a wonderful country,' I thought. 'But I just hope I'm not called to be a missionary there. Too many never come back!'

Now I was finding the reports coming out of China thrilling. 'One day,' wrote Brother Andrew, in his magazine *Open Doors*, 'perhaps quite soon, someone will write about this revival, and we shall advertise the book.' As I read those words, a voice within said, 'You do it!' I was taken completely by surprise. Never had I received such a sudden and unexpected commission. Was it really God?

At this point, God and I had a little altercation. Who was I to write such a book? What did I really know

Pastor Hsi (1836–1896);
'An apostolic man.'

about China anyway? I had never been there—I was never likely to go there—and so on. There's one sure thing about arguing with God, he always wins! Within a couple of months I was in China.

'It is almost impossible for anyone who has not lived and worked in China to understand the actual situation there, much less write a book about the subject!' That was the pointed comment made to me by a 'China Expert' on learning that I was writing this book. I had to agree, although I felt like saying, 'You had better take that up with God.' In fact, as soon as I had come to terms with what God was asking me to do I began to understand what was to be the nature of the book.

In order to understand something of what is happening now in China, it has proved necessary to give a brief outline of China's history, how the church was planted, and how it has fared under Communism. However, I have come to see that what has been happening in mainland China has significance, not for that country only, but for the church of God worldwide, especially in the West. It seemed that God was there chalking up things in bold Chinese characters, that he wanted me to convey to his people in the free world. They concern truths of great importance as this present age moves on to its climax.

Just to handle the material has done something for me. I can never be quite the same again. Often my manuscript has been wet with tears—not tears of sadness or sentimentality or sympathy, but of awe, of wonder, of sheer admiration for the grace of God at work in mortal flesh. Out of the melting has come worship. My God, how great you are! If others' hearts are also melted as they read—not to cool and solidify again in the old mould, but to be poured into a new mould of God's choosing—the book will have accomplished its aim.

Chapter Two

HEIGHTS AND DEPTHS

For I am convinced that neither death nor life, neither angels nor demons, neither the present nor the future ... neither height nor depth, nor anything else in all creation, will be able to separate us from the love of God that is in Christ Jesus our Lord.

Romans 8:38–39

China is the oldest civilization in the world. In its long and turbulent history spanning fifty centuries, it has scaled the heights of success and achievement, and plummeted to the depths of defeat and humiliation. Excavations in North-Central China uncovered a highly developed civilization with its own written language that existed almost 2,000 years before Christ. About the time of Moses (1500 B.C.) the Chinese were wearing furs and silks, producing beautiful works of art, erecting elaborate buildings, and going to war in wheeled chariots. In 1000 B.C. they had a national university in their capital city, and were using a compass to chart their journeys.

It was the Qin (Ch'in)[1] dynasty (255–206 B.C.) that gave the nation its name, China, and its first Emperor, Qin Shihuang. He in turn gave China for the first time a unified written language. It would seem that Chairman Mao Zedong drew much inspiration for many of his ideas from this powerful and successful ruler. As a barricade against the nomadic barbarians who lived on the borders of China, Shi built the Great Wall. Some sections had been built earlier, but he linked them all together, and constructed guard towers every few hundred yards. It was built largely by slave labour and thousands of the workers perished in the course of its construction. It stretched for 1,500 miles along the western border of China. Built of stone, brick and earth, it was twenty feet in height, had a road on top fifteen feet wide and was garrisoned by a quarter of a million soldiers.

For more than 3,600 years China was ruled by a succession of dynasties. The Ming dynasty (1368–1644) was especially famous for its architecture, furniture, paintings and pottery. Not far from where I used to live in the south-west of England, a representative of Sothebys, the famous auctioneers, spotted a small porcelain jar serving as a flower-pot in a lady's garden. He advised her to have it valued. It was found to be a very rare fifteenth century Imperial Ming. It was subsequently auctioned for a modest quarter of a million pounds!

It was China, with its great love of learning and scholarship, who gave us paper in A.D. 105, and the first dictionary, with 10,000 characters. So great was their respect for learning that for centuries they would never throw away a piece of paper with writing on it. It had to be burned in a special receptacle. In Britain the use of fingerprints as a method of identification goes back to about 1880. The Chinese use of them for this purpose goes back to 700 A.D.! About 1000 A.D. they invented gunpowder, used at first to make firecrackers to scare off evil spirits. It was during this period they discovered a vaccine for smallpox and produced the first reference book on medicine. The Chinese certainly made a unique contribution to the progress of civilization, especially in its earliest centuries.

'Zhongguo' is the Chinese for China, and means 'the middle country'. In Chinese thinking China is 'the middle', centre of the world. Beyond their borders were the inferior races, the outsiders and the barbarians. This national pride and self-centredness caused them to treat with disdain all that was going on in the big developing world outside. When Lord Macartney headed a diplomatic mission to the Manchu Emperor in 1793, eager to find a market in China for British goods, he received a pretty cool reception. The Emperor sent a letter to King George III: 'As your ambassador can see for himself, we possess all things. I set no value on objects strange or ingenious, and have no use for your country's manufactures.'

Confucianism was another factor in their isolationist policy. A philosophy more than a religion, it had for centuries bred in the Chinese an attitude of resistance to change. All this, together with an inborn fear and hatred of foreigners from whom they had suffered much, had cut China off from the rest of the world. Consequently she got left behind in the race of human progress. At the beginning of the eighteen-hundreds, China was still a closed land to foreigners. It was soon, however, to be prised open in a way that would leave this proud and cultured nation shamed and humiliated. For this the western powers, and Britain in particular, must bear the prime responsibility. It is a phase of colonial history which we may prefer to forget. Here seeds were sown which were to bear fruit in the rise and triumph of Chinese Marxism.

The Portuguese were the first to see the potential of marketing Chinese goods in Europe. They secured an island off the coast of China, called Macau, which they still hold. Early in the eighteenth century, opium smoking was becoming a social menace in China, through the drug being smuggled into the country from India and Turkey. Portugal saw how this lucrative, though immoral trade, could be the means of financing her exports to Europe.

It was not long before Britain too saw the trading potential of Chinese goods in Europe. In response to British overtures, China had made it clear that she was not interested in buying British goods, now flowing from the industrial revolution. If China did not want her exports, how could Britain finance the purchase of Chinese tea and silks? Only, it would seem, by following the despicable example of the Portuguese and getting involved in opium smuggling. All this was done with the knowledge and connivance of the British government.

Through the powerful East India Trading Company, operating under the patronage of the British government, the illegal traffic greatly increased, to the alarm of the Chinese government. The British parliament seemed to have no qualms about trading opium, at least not to the Chinese. It was only the smuggling aspect of it that seemed to trouble the British conscience. It needed to be legalized. But the Chinese were not interested in negotiating a free trade agreement. They were fighting to curb this nefarious traffic that was bringing such misery to their people.

When the Chinese adopted a get-tough policy, the British navy became involved, and fighting broke out. China was to pay dearly for daring to resist the exploitation of her people. It took two Opium Wars to bring

China finally to her knees. The first was concluded in 1842 with the Treaty of Nanking. This required China to surrender to the British the Island of Hong Kong, and to permit foreigners to reside for the purpose of trade or other legitimate activities in 'the five Treaty Ports' on the China coast. These foreigners were to have special rights. They could only be tried for criminal offences by courts composed of their own nationals, not by Chinese courts of law—a terrible humiliation for the Chinese nation.

The second Opium War which broke out in 1856 ended with the sacking of Beijing (Peking) by European troops and the signing of the Treaty of Tientsin in 1860. This gave Britain further territory on the mainland opposite Hong Kong, called The New Territories—due to be returned to China, together with the island of Hong Kong in 1997. In addition, further treaty ports were to be opened, there was to be freedom for foreigners to travel anywhere in China, and the opium trade was legalized. 'The Unequal Treaties' as they came to be called, were deeply resented. This was the beginning of the rape of China by the West.

If Britain was the main culprit in doing 'the dirty work', the other major powers must share her guilt. As China lay prostrate and bleeding, they gathered round to take their share of the spoil. It is not without significance that the first shots of the Opium War were fired by British naval ships on the Chinese war junks between Hong Kong Island and Kowloon on the mainland, two territories that are shortly to be handed back to mainland China. Again, it is not without significance that the western nations that greedily participated in illegal drug trafficking now have a drug problem of massive proportions that they cannot control. 'You reap what you sow' is true of nations as well as of individuals.

Another unfortunate aspect of the opium racket was the fact that the first Protestant missionaries to China were from the same nation, Britain, that was condoning this opium smuggling. It was only through the good offices of the British East India Company that western missionaries could at first gain entry to the country. So, in the minds of many Chinese 'foreign devils' (Westerners), 'foreign mud' (as they called opium) and foreign religion were all of a piece.

Writing from the Chinese port of Swatow in 1856 Hudson Taylor, the pioneer missionary, recounted the following: 'Not less than 32,000 pounds of opium enter China every month at this port alone, the cost of which is about a quarter of a million sterling. After this you will not be surprised to learn that the people are wretchedly poor, ignorant and vicious.' Later he wrote, not surprisingly, 'The people have no love for foreigners.'

It was throughout this traumatic period of Chinese history that those early Christian pioneers were laying the foundations of the church in China. 'The calibre of these early missionaries was often of the highest order. Scholars, linguists, doctors and teachers came using their skills, thus preparing the way for the spread of the gospel.'[2] We must salute these heralds of the cross, who at enormous sacrifice, sometimes life itself, blazed a trail right into the heart of China. Later we shall have cause to consider the strengths and weaknesses of that early missionary movement in the light of what is now taking place, but their dedication and self-sacrifice can never be questioned.

The dawn of the twentieth century found China weak and vulnerable. The incursions of the West had greatly weakened her and after centuries of isolation she was in no way ready to take her place alongside other world powers. The Imperial Manchu government, the dynasty that had ruled China for 260 years, was inefficient and corrupt. It came to an end when the Emperor was forced to resign in 1911.

The years that followed the formation of a Republican government in China proved to be tempestuous ones, witnessing radical changes, and preparing the way for the establishing of the People's Republic of China in 1949.

If we are to have an understanding of the two kingdoms that are now vieing for the hearts of the Chinese, the one that is temporal and the one that is eternal, we must look more carefully at this fascinating and formative period of thirty-eight years. We may be surprised to discover that at the very inception of the Chinese Republic there were strong Christian as well as socialistic influences at work. Let us then take a few pages to look back at the seed bed of the Communist Revolution.

Chapter Three

THE SKY IS RED

It is God who judges: He brings one down, he exalts another.

Psalm 75:7

While dynastic rule was in its death throes, a leader appeared on the political scene with the vision of a China, strong and free. Dr Sun Yat-sen, although Chinese-born, had spent much of his youth in Hawaii. He had travelled widely both in America and Europe. Not only had he been influenced by the principles of parliamentary democracy, but by the socialistic ideas of men like Karl Marx. He had a consuming passion to see a free and prosperous China, and his fertile mind was ever searching for answers to the nation's urgent social and economic problems. Although he had no prior experience or training in government, he was dedicated to the overthrow of the Manchu Dynasty.

Travelling overseas, Sun raised funds from Chinese expatriates, and was involved in several abortive attempts to overthrow the Imperial government. A high price was placed on his head. The climate was ripe for change, if not for revolution. Most Chinese were convinced that the government was corrupt, but few had any clear idea of what was the right course to take.

As a politician, Sun was something of a hybrid. He was committed to constitutional democracy while holding socialist ideas on the regulation of capital and land reform. Probably his vision was to combine a democratic form of government with socialistic principles for the economy. Consequently Dr Sun Yat-sen is acclaimed by the Nationalists as the instigator of democracy in China, and by the Communists as their first revolutionary. A revolutionary he was, but not a Marxist. 'The reason the revolution succeeded,' he declared, 'was because I relied totally on God's help.' That is not the confession of a Marxist.

Dr Sun was evidently a committed Christian. Speaking in a church in Boston, USA, in 1912 he declared,

> Men say that the revolution originated with me. I do not deny the charge. But where did the idea of revolution come from? It came because, from my youth, I was brought in touch with foreign missionaries. Those from Europe and America with whom I associated put the ideals of freedom and liberty in my heart. Now I call upon the church to help in the establishment of the new government. The Republic cannot endure unless there is that virtue, righteousness, at the centre of the nation's life.

In a letter to old friends of his in Hong Kong, he wrote on the occasion of his election to the presidency, 'I thank you for your earnest prayers on my behalf. I am glad to tell you that we are going to have religious toleration in China, and I assure you that Christianity will flourish under the new regime.' Dr Sun's son, a number of his cabinet colleagues, and his private secretary were all committed Christians. It was amazing to find that the gospel of Christ had penetrated to the highest levels of government.

October 10th 1911, called in China 'The Double Tenth', is still viewed as the birth of the Revolution. An army unit revolted, the Imperial palace was attacked, and not long after the Emperor abdicated. Dr Sun, who was overseas raising funds, hurried back to China, and on New Year's Day 1912 was inaugurated as the first president of the Republic.

Sun's initial tenure of office was very brief. A power struggle followed and he was ousted. Control in China fell into the hands of a number of warlords, and it was not until ten years later that he was able to grasp again the reins of leadership.

Meanwhile a series of significant events had taken place that were to have a profound effect on China and shape the type of government that would come out of the Chinese melting pot. The first of these events took place in Russia. It was the Bolshevik Revolution of 1917. Initially this had little impact on China. The new Republican government was not looking to Russia for answers.

The next event came with the conclusion of World War One, in which China had sided with the Allies. On conclusion of hostilities (1918) she was fully expecting that Chinese territory held by Germany would be restored to her. Assurances to this effect had been given by Woodrow Wilson, the American President. In the event —when the Versailles Treaty was concluded in 1919— this territory was given to Japan who had captured it from the Germans during the war.

This was a devastating blow to China, and produced deep resentment and widespread political reaction. For many Chinese, faith in democracy and the West was shattered, and many eyes were turned towards Russia and the Bolshevik Revolution for a solution to China's problems. Russia was more than willing to respond and move into the vacuum created by the Treaty of Versailles. Marxism became Russia's big export to China, and Comintern agents were trained in Moscow to incite rebellion and to form Communist cells. It was as a result of this activity that in 1921 the Chinese Communist Party was formed.

A nationalistic fervour now took over in China that the nation had never witnessed before. Two forces emerged, each making its bid to lead the nation into a new day of prosperity and liberty. One advocated democracy, science and modern education, and called for the renunciation of the ancient traditional culture. The other, finding its inspiration in the Bolshevik Revolution, believed that Marxism was the answer. Both now turned to Sun Yat-sen as the only man who could harmonize these two conflicting ideals and unite the nation. He proposed a democratic form of government that advocated aspects of Marxism in its economic programme and the handling of land ownership.

Probably Dr Sun's greatest miscalculation was to assume that western democracy could be immediately introduced to China when there was no foundation for this. Professor C.P. Fitzgerald has pointed out that in Chinese thinking, 'There is no place for freedom as the West understands it, no place for salvation as the Christian understands it, and no place for individualism as the liberal would have it.' Given time, there was little doubt which way the pendulum would swing.

Dr Sun's re-election to the presidency in 1922 was short-lived. He died in 1925. The conflicting ideologies to which he had been subjected, some of which he had embraced, never robbed him of his faith. On his death bed he declared, 'I am a disciple of Jesus Christ, commissioned by God to declare war against evil. Even when I die, I want people to know I am a Christian.'

A young army officer, also possessing Christian convictions, had become Sun's right hand man. His name was Chiang Kai-shek. He had been to Moscow, and like Sun, had been influenced initially by Marxism. Dr Sun's mantle now came to rest on him. The Nationalist Kuomintang government that he now headed up decided to continue Sun's policies. The situation that they faced was not just one of change, or of transition, but of revolution, and the tasks for the new government were enormous.

By 1927, though the Nationalists had broken with the Communists, they had made considerable progress in re-unifying the country. Then Mao Zedong marshalled his Peasant army, based at this time in South-East China, and commenced his famous Long March to the steppes of the North-West. This, described more fully in the following chapter, is one of the great epics of Chinese history. There he established a secure base from which to conduct his struggle against the Nationalist forces.

It was at this point that a new danger appeared. The Japanese had seized Manchuria and were now threatening China. War with Japan broke out in 1937 and dragged on for eight weary years. The need was urgent for Nationalists and Communists to stand against the common foe. Each accused the other of not doing so. At Mao's instigation they buried the hatchet for the time being at least and concentrated on resisting the foreign invader. China was eventually saved by the Allies, who defeated Japan in World War Two.

In 1946 civil war between the Nationalists and the Communists broke out in earnest. It was a life and death struggle and lasted from 1946 to 1949, costing more lives, it is reckoned, than any war of modern times. Slowly and inexorably the Communists pushed back the numerically superior Nationalist forces until they had all been driven from mainland China to find a refuge in Taiwan (Formosa). Then, on a bleak February morning in 1949 the Communist divisions marched into Beijing (Peking), and the crimson flag with its five stars was unfurled. Soon after, China's new ruler, Chairman Mao Zedong (Mau Tse-tung) proclaimed from the Gate of Heavenly Peace in Beijing (Peking) the birth of The People's Republic of China.

Chapter Four

THE GREAT HELMSMAN

*All men are like grass, and all their glory is like
the flowers of the field. The grass withers and the
flowers fall, because the breath of the Lord blows
on them .... but the word of our God stands for
ever.*

Isaiah 40:6–8

We cannot really understand China today without
looking at the man who, more than any other, has
shaped the nation. Mao Zedong (Mao Tse-tung) was
rightly called 'The Great Helmsman'. To the young
revolutionaries of China he embodied all the ideals of
the Revolution, and they venerated him as though he
were God. Whatever we may think of his political philosophy and his ruthless methods, no one can deny the
magnitude of his achievement in uniting and galvan-
izing a dismembered and dispirited nation—the largest
on the face of the earth—giving them pride in their
nationhood, giving them a universal simplified script
and bringing them 'out of the Middle Ages into the
nuclear era', as one of the foremost Communist states of
the twentieth century.

Disillusioned with western liberalism, he embraced

Chairman Mao Zedong.

Marxism, which he proceeded to adapt to the Chinese situation. It was his conviction that China must find its own form of Marxism. He was one of the twelve founding members of the Chinese Communist Party formed in 1921, although not at that time the leader. When Chiang Kai-shek took over leadership of the government on the death of Sun Yat-sen, he co-operated at first with the new leader, but there was no prospect of any lasting alliance. While promoting a united front with Chiang, the Communists had other plans afoot. They commenced to organize a peasant army of Communist guerillas (1924–25). When the inevitable break came with Chiang, they knew that they had to build up their forces, or the superior Nationalist army would overwhelm them.

Based at that time in South-East China, the Communists decided to make a strategic retreat to the mountains of the North-West. This involved a trek of some 6,000 miles, the crossing of eighteen mountain ranges and twenty-four rivers, and lasted from 1934 to 1936. Throughout this incredible journey, known as The Long March, the Communist forces were constantly harassed by the Nationalists, and greatly reduced through sickness and casualties. Even today, the Chinese consider the feat of The Long March to be one of the proudest moments in their long history. It inspired many young Chinese to join the Communist Party.

It was while on The Long March that Mao's position as the leader of the Communists was established. At this point he decided to break away from his dependence on Stalin and to plough his own furrow. Having reached his objective, Mao set up his new revolutionary base. The following year Mao's systematic studies of Marxist philosophy began to be published. Later his followers were to describe him as 'the greatest genius of

our time', and *Mao's Thoughts* as 'the greatest truth ever
known since time immemorial'. In a two year period
two billion copies of his writings rolled off the press.
This all helped in the deifying of Mao. Yet with his
decline and death, the Mao legend was to fade and
wither like the flower of the field.

The ultimate victory of the Communists over Chiang
Kai-shek's forces in 1949 was a tremendous feat,
achieved against all odds. Perhaps the major reason
was that the Communists had a vision, a cause and an
ideal that they felt was worth fighting for and worth
dying for. The Nationalists did not. The Communists
were excited about their vision, they had faith in its
fulfilment, and so they went about seeking to 'convert'
others to their cause. Here is an obvious lesson for
professing Christians.

China is essentially a peasant nation tied to tradition,
especially that of Confucianism. There was a strong
bond between ruler and subject, father and son, and
husband and wife. Although Mao set himself to improve
the lot of the peasants, he felt that these bonds, together
with those of religion, capitalism and autocracy, were
the major obstacles in the establishing of a new Marxist
society, and so he set out to destroy them.

Such radical social changes are seldom effected without violent conflict. Mao not only accepted this, it was a
vital element in his Communistic philosophy. 'Revolution is an act of violence whereby one class overthrows
the authority of another. Revolution is not a dinner
party.'

Mao was a great visionary and revolutionary thinker,
but he was no economist. To him the great thing was to
maintain the revolutionary spirit, and to abide by his
own Marxist dogmas. Whether the things he had
initiated were really workable seemed only a secondary

consideration. In the years that followed he embarked
upon a series of adventurous policies, all of which proved
more or less disastrous. This undermined people's confidence, as well as resulting in a great deal of suffering
and bitterness.

In the years 1950–52, Mao commenced to wipe out
the landlord class. This involved the liquidation of an
estimated 800,000 people and the giving of their land to
the peasants. In 1958 the land was taken from them for
state-owned communes. These could encompass several
towns with up to 100,000 people in each. Private ownership was ended and all was centrally organized. This
experiment was something of a disaster, and the communes have now been dismantled in China.

The next policy was *The Hundred Flowers Movement* in
1956 in which Mao encouraged intellectuals to criticize
government policy. The party was shocked by the
strength and outspokenness of the response. It led to an
immediate crackdown on the intellectuals. Many of
them were shipped to Mongolia, the 'Siberia' of China,
Tibet and other remote regions, and some of them were
never heard of again. Criticism of the government
became an act of high treason. This volte-face was
another severe blow to the people's confidence in the
integrity of Mao and his policies.

Then came *The Great Leap Forward* in 1958. The purpose here was to turn China into a vast industrial-
agricultural nation, that would be able to compete with
the major nations of the world. In his attempt to produce
'instant success', Mao planned to break up the family
unit, which had always been the great strength of the
Chinese society. Families were divided up and sent off to
form communes. Such a vast undertaking could never
be accomplished overnight, and The Great Leap was
doomed to failure from the start. Two successive years

of drought and flooding sealed its fate. According to Chinese government admission ten million peasants died in the famine. US statistics reckon it was twenty million. At this point Mao became a target for strong criticism within the party.

After a period in semi-seclusion, the revolutionary spirit of The Great Helmsman began to stir again. Was he afraid that power was slipping from his hands for good? He was certainly afraid of 'revisionism'—that the nation would lose its revolutionary spirit and slide back into moderation and liberalization. Behind the backs of the men in power he planned a personal comeback, to mobilize the youth, and to revive the revolutionary spirit. This movement came to be called *The Great Cultural Revolution* and proved to be the biggest disaster of all.

By-passing both the army and the party, none of which he could fully trust, Mao took his case directly to the youth of the country. He ordered all schools to be closed. He addressed a million Red Guards in Beijing (Peking), commissioning them to travel through the nation destroying old ideas, customs, habits, crushing all who were thought to be taking the Capitalist road.

The Revolution almost became a riot. Houses were looted, the elderly insulted, and innocent people condemned. To denounce someone as a Capitalist was an easy way to settle old scores. The young Red Guards were often totally undisciplined. It is said that a million illegitimate babies were born during this period. Priceless art treasures were destroyed. Churches, even those operating under the authority of the government, and all other religious buildings were closed. The Chinese church went through a winter of desolation. There was soon a strong reaction against the ruthless behaviour of these young revolutionaries. Rival groups sprang up within the Red Guard movement. Pitched battles occurred and a general state of disorder prevailed.

Meanwhile farming had been neglected and the economy was moving towards a precipice of disaster. Mao admitted that the Red Guards had not fulfilled his high expectations of them, and the army was called in to restore order.

The revolution had by now touched the highest echelons of government. Even President Liu Shaoqi, Mao's appointed successor, was publicly humiliated and branded as a 'lackey of Imperialism'. He was dismissed from the party and died in prison some years later.

The Red Guards were dedicated to boost the image of Mao to the point where he was virtually deified. At first they erected his portrait in every public place. They waved the *Little Red Book* and chanted Mao Thoughts. But when the reaction set in, all this began to disappear from the scene. Mao's young henchmen had thoroughly discredited him. Many of them were sent home in disgrace, or sent away to work on communes. In the words of a distinguished Communist Party writer, 'The Great Cultural Revolution was the greatest revolution that sent culture to its death.' It is doubtful whether Mao's image in the thinking of the Chinese people ever recovered from this debacle.

Contemporary with Mao was another man who made a notable contribution to the shaping of The People's Republic, Zhou Enlai (Chou En-lai). He was appointed Premier when the Republic was founded in 1949, a position which he held until his death, a few months before that of Mao. An outstanding diplomat, highly respected internationally and loved by the Chinese people, he acted to restrain the extremists in the Cultural Revolution. It was largely through his diplomatic initiative that China was admitted to the United Nations in 1971. It was he who invited the USA to send a table-tennis team to China—'Ping-Pong Diplomacy'—which led to the visit of President Nixon and the eventual resumption of diplomatic relations with America.

The difference in the political outlook of Mao and Zhou became all too clear in their later years. It represented a tension that is reflected today in the struggle for power within the Chinese Communist party. It is the conflict between the leftists or dogmatists and the pragmatists. Mao was a dogmatist, who was wedded to the Marxist dogma, from which there could be no deviation. His ideology blinded him to the fact that his theories were not working and would never work. Zhou on the other hand was a pragmatist, with his feet firmly on the ground. If a political theory was not producing results it must be modified or scrapped.

The pragmatists see no hope of China ever competing with the major nations of the world without the easing of controls and modernization. There must be freedom for initiative and enterprise. Workers need more than revolutionary ideals, they must have financial incentives, if output is to increase. The nation needs modernizing if its vast resources are to be harnessed to the building of a strong and prosperous China. That means opening the country to the techniques and expertise of the West.

The leftists see these trends as highly dangerous. When the people get a taste of liberty and prosperity, they no longer turn up to the Party meeting to study Marxism. They lose their revolutionary zeal. To allow the people to fraternize freely with foreigners, would open them to the decadent influences of the West. The Party would lose its tight control over the people. The nation would slide back into Capitalism.

These opposing viewpoints are reflected, first by the

slogan of the pragmatists, 'It doesn't matter what colour the cat is, as long as it catches mice.' And the retort of the Leftists, 'It doesn't matter if the cat catches mice or not, as long as it is red!' This is the big dilemma now facing Chinese Communism.

In July 1976 'The Great Helmsman' died, leaving a dispirited and disillusioned nation. Here are the words of a youth by the name of Mo-min who wrote in one of China's newspapers:

The word 'tomorrow' has been a word of great fascination to me. When I was attending primary school, 'The Great Leap Forward' was the dream of tomorrow: we were going to live happily in prosperity. But what did we get? Disasters!

And then The Cultural Revolution: tomorrow means total liberation, and we shall conquer the world. What did we get? Disasters! Now the young people of China cannot help but learn this lesson: Don't hope too much! Don't be optimistic! Don't think about tomorrow!

Here are the concluding remarks on Mao by an able student of the China scene: 'If he had died some twenty-five years earlier, he would most certainly have gone down in Chinese history as one of the greatest Chinese reformers. As it was, he lived long enough to thoroughly destroy his own hard-won reputation.'[3]

On his death-bed Mao appointed Hua Guofeng as his successor, although in fact the power was already in the hands of 'The Gang of Four'. This consisted of his widow, Jiang Qing—who had her sights set on the Chairmanship—and her three colleagues. How much this was the result of Mao's connivance, and how much due to the fact that he was too old to do anything about it, is not clear, but in the eyes of many Chinese Mao's crowning failure was his inability to restrain his ambitious wife. As one writer put it, 'Without Mao, there would have been no Madam Mao.' The suspicion of Mao's complicity was expressed in one of the famous wall posters that spoke of 'The Gang of Five'!

It was this group of political schemers who dominated the closing years of the Mao era. In the period of unrest that followed the Chairman's death, The Gang of Four were arrested and eventually tried and imprisoned. The leader who eventually emerged was Deng Xiaoping. Though he declined to take the official position of Chairman or Premier, preferring to lead from behind, he was clearly the new strong man of China. He now began to turn the nation in a completely new direction. He introduced the *Four Modernizations Programme* aimed at agriculture, industry, defence and science.

From 1978 it seemed that even the Bamboo Curtain was lifting. China entered a phase of liberty that it had not enjoyed since the Communists came to power. Foreign guests became a familiar sight in the streets of China's major cities. Young Chinese were able to go overseas to study. Business enterprises sprang up. People called it 'The Second Liberation'.

A wall in Beijing (Peking) became world-famous as posters were plastered up that in a subtle way disclosed the thinking of many Chinese regarding 'the feudalism' of the Mao era and the longing for greater freedom. It is said that Deng Xiaoping instigated the Big Poster Campaign on 'Democracy Wall'. However, this opportunity for free expression went 'over the top', and the leadership was compelled to put a stop to what could have become a popular revolt.

Deng's progressive economic measures came into serious trouble, and his liberalization was thought to be resulting in too much crime, and was opening the nation to the decadence of the West. So, early in the eighties,

Deng Xiaoping.

the pendulum began to swing the other way, in one of those predictable reversals of policy which the Chinese have learned to expect. Thankfully, there was no return to the savage oppression of the Cultural Revolution. Nevertheless there was a significant tightening of control in a way typical of a Marxist state.

Deng now launched the 'Anti Crime Campaign', resulting in an estimated 100,000 arrests and 10,000 executions. This was followed by the Anti Spiritual Pollution Campaign, aimed at countering liberalizing tendencies, especially those coming in from outside. This became in some quarters an excuse for attacking the unofficial house churches. Finally there was the Part Rectification Campaign, which appeared to be Deng's effort to purge from the Party those who held strong Leftist positions, so that he could proceed with pragmatic policies.

What of the future? The most knowledgeable are wisely the most reluctant to predict. Deng is in his eighties. He may no longer be around by the time you read this. Who will follow him, and in what direction will he lead China? How reassuring to know that these decisions are not in fact in the hands of man. 'The authorities that exist have been established by God.'[4]

The reader will be eager to know how all this has affected and is affecting the church of Jesus Christ. First, we must go back and see how the church was planted in China and how it has been faring in a Marxist society.

Chapter Five

PLANTING THE CHURCH

*The kingdom of heaven is like a mustard seed,
which a man took and planted in his field. Though
it is the smallest of all your seeds, yet when it
grows, it is the largest of garden plants and
becomes a tree, so that the birds of the air come
and perch in its branches.*

Matthew 13:31–32

The first to sow the seeds of Christianity in China were
Nestorians who came from Persia and built churches
and monasteries. Later came Catholic missionaries.
They did not preach a truly saving message and never
succeeded in making the faith indigenous to China.
With the overthrow of the Mongols, Christianity was
'sunk almost without trace'.

In 1579 the Roman Catholic Church made a fresh
start to establish the faith in China. Jesuit missionaries
came from the Portuguese colony of Macau, just off the
coast of South China. They were eventually forbidden
to preach by the Emperor when they took a stand
against ancestral worship. There was a mass exodus of
priests, and again the light of the Christian faith was all
but extinguished.

Robert Morrison (1782–1834).
The first Protestant missionary to China.

In 1807 Robert Morrison, a young Scot with the London Missionary Society, set sail for China with the burning desire to lead the Chinese people to Christ. The problem was how to gain entry, since the British East India Company were the door-keepers, and they were scared of missionary activity affecting their trade with China. Eventually Morrison arrived in Macau, where he settled down to translate the Scriptures into Chinese, a task which he finally accomplished some eighteen years later. The problem with this translation, as well as that of another by a Dr Marshman, was that it was in the classical style used by scholars but not understood by the common people. Nevertheless, both the translations were a tremendous achievement of missionary endeavour.

Later, after some hesitation, Morrison accepted an appointment as translator to the East India Company, simply to gain entrance to his beloved China. Thus it was that Christian missionaries and the iniquitous opium trade carried on by the East India Company were to be for ever linked in the minds of the Chinese. As we have seen, the two treaties of 1842 and 1860, forced China to open her doors to the West, both for free trade and for missionary activity.

The China Inland Mission under the leadership of Hudson Taylor had been newly formed, as well as other missionary agencies. In the years that followed there came to China from the West, first a trickle, then a swelling stream of dedicated missionaries.

Those early servants of God in China were not to know that in less than a hundred years, every Christian missionary would be evacuated from the mainland, with little prospect of the door reopening. The church of Jesus Christ that they were to establish in that land was to go through its baptism of fire, which would test to the

*Robert Morrison (1772–1834)
translating the Scriptures with two Chinese assistants.*

utmost the quality of the work, and reveal its strengths and its weaknesses.

There is no question as to the dedication of those early missionaries and the tremendous sacrifices that they gladly made for the cause of Christ. Many of them were highly trained and gifted. Of all nations, the Chinese set a high value on scholarship and culture, and this worked in favour of the early missionary effort. In other respects, however, events were heavily weighted against them. In the beginning they had gained entry, as we have already observed, through the discredited colonial policies of Britain and the West. It has been said, 'Opium traffic was the single greatest impediment to Christianity in China in the nineteenth century.'

Having experienced for centuries the cruelty of the foreign invader, the Chinese looked upon the activity of all foreigners with the greatest suspicion. No wonder the ambassador of the cross was viewed as 'a foreign devil', and any Chinese who embraced his doctrine as a 'half-foreigner'. This whole attitude was to strengthen the arm of the Communists when they came to power determined to drive out all foreign missionaries from the the land. They did not need to think up 'a case' against foreign missionaries. The colonial policies of Britain and the West provided them with all the ammunition that they required. The fact that the missionaries themselves had been totally opposed to the opium trade and the fact that it was eventually committed Christians in the British parliament who fought successfully to have the traffic stopped, did not absolve Christianity of its guilt in the eyes of the Communists.

On the other side of the coin, poor Chinese, who hadn't much to lose anyway by associating with foreigners, could respond to the gospel for the wrong motives. To them, the missionary was always wealthy, and he occupied a position of privilege in the land. The temptation to be a 'rice Christian' who professed faith for material advantage, was accentuated by the fact that the treaties secured by the West offered benefits for Christian converts.

The other weakness of the early missionary effort, like that of the Nestorians and the Catholics before them, was that it imposed western forms of worship and culture upon the Chinese that were totally foreign to them. Most of the early missionary organizations failed to see

Hudson Taylor (1832–1905).
From a portrait by an aunt, painted in 1852.

Hudson Taylor (1832–1905)
in middle life.

that if the church was ever to root naturally in the soil of China, it needed to be divested of its western forms.

Among those early pioneers, Hudson Taylor was the exception in this respect, for he encouraged his missionaries to adopt Chinese dress and identify in every possible way with the Chinese culture. He sought to raise up national leadership and hand over to those leaders as soon as they were capable of taking over. But for this he heaped upon himself much abuse and criticism from other missionaries.

Another great weakness was that missionary organizations generally established their churches on denominational lines. The Church of Christ in China was the amalgamation of several denominations, each retaining its own distinctive identity. Even the China Inland Mission, which in so many other respects had adapted to Chinese culture, distributed its workers over the various provinces according to their denominational identity, each church retaining its own particular form of church government. An Anglican bishop was appointed over the Anglican churches. In this way the tragic divisions of western Christendom were exported to China.

In the period of unrest that marked the closing years of Imperial rule, there was a violent outbreak of anti-foreign and anti-missionary feeling. It was The Boxer Rebellion of 1900 which was designed to drive out the foreigner with his political, social and religious traditions. Although it only lasted for a year, its effects were devastating. It almost brought the great missionary venture to a tragic end. Foreigners in large centres were more easily protected, but missionaries, in isolated situations, were particularly vulnerable. Nearly 200 Protestant missionaries and their dependants died, and the Roman Catholic losses were even heavier. Christian leaders among the Chinese suffered greatly too. There were amazing stories of heroism and loyalty as the Chinese church faced this terrible ordeal. It was a foretaste of what was to happen on a much wider scale when the Communists took over.

With the dawn of the twentieth century we reach a fascinating phase in the story of the planting of the church in China. God is never limited to what we consider are 'the proper channels'. He has his own ways of working. China has a long history of spontaneous and indigenous movements of the Spirit. Some of these revival

John Sung (1901–1944).
'The Flaming Evangelist.'

movements were God's way of cleansing and purifying his people, and filling them with the power of the Holy Spirit. It was so with the revivals under the ministry of the Canadian missionary, Jonathan Goforth, which took place first in Manchuria (1908), followed by outbreaks in other parts of China.

There were other revivals where the emphasis was decidedly evangelistic, with the powerful preaching of the gospel, and many turning to Christ. John Sung, whose ministry was not confined to China, was mightily used in the period prior to the Communist takeover. This eccentric preacher was only forty-two when he died, but he turned thousands to Christ. He has been described as 'the greatest evangelist China has ever known'.

There was the great pastor-preacher Wang Mingdao who drew thousands to his church in Beijing (Peking), and who stood as a bastion of righteousness, when other Chinese leaders compromised with the authorities. We shall hear more of him later.

It is significant that before the Communists came to power there were a number of indigenous movements which were in different ways an attempt to restructure and revitalize the body of Christ. They were recovery movements that restored certain aspects of truth— springs that broke out that would eventually flow into and comingle with the main stream of the house church movement in China.

The first to gain prominence was *The True Jesus Church* established by Paul Wei in Tianjin (Tientsin) and Beijing (Peking) in the year 1917. They emphasized witnessing, tithing and local church government. They were at home with spiritual gifts, speaking in tongues, exercising healing and deliverance, and experiencing other manifestations of God's power. Communal living was also a feature of their lifestyle in the early days.

Their churches sprang up throughout China and amongst Chinese overseas.

By 1949, when the Communists had taken over, their membership was reported to be 125,000. Compare this with The Church of Christ in China, the union of several major denominations already mentioned, with a membership of 196,000 after a hundred years of missionary effort. Denominational structures do not facilitate, but rather hinder swift expansion. When churches free themselves from this yoke they tend to make more rapid growth. But there are dangers if a movement becomes exclusive and The True Jesus Church did not escape this hazard, so that later on some excesses and divisions marred the testimony.

Another remarkable movement was that of *The Little Flock* that began in 1926 under the leadership of Watchman Nee, whose Chinese name was Nee To-sheng, the surname being placed first. Through his books, almost all written by others from his sermon notes, he is the most well-known Chinese Christian in the West. For a short time he had association with the Exclusive Brethren, though he did not initially draw his insight from them. In fact, when he visited one of their churches in Britain, and was asked by his host 'What do you think of our assembly?' he replied, 'Very nice, very nice, brother,' and then shaking his head slowly, he added, 'But no good for casting out demons in China!' Watchman Nee and his fellow workers knew the necessity of the empowering of the Holy Spirit.

He had no time for formality and churchianity. He was critical of the current missionary movement and the way in which the Chinese church had become dependent on the West. He took the New Testament, as many others had done before him, as providing all the principles needed for New Testament life and practice.

He saw the founding of churches as being a ministry of apostolic men who were itinerant, and to be distinguished from the local pastors and teachers.

Inevitably he drew upon himself a flood of criticism from the missionary movement, particularly when some missionaries, and even whole churches founded by missionaries, joined The Little Flock, but his work grew and prospered, even after the Communists had taken over. In twenty years the movement numbered 700 churches with more than 70,000 members.

Some division occurred in The Little Flock shortly before the Communist takeover. After the arrest of Watchman Nee, his colleague, Witness Li, then based in Taiwan (Formosa), became the dominant leader, but the direction of his leadership did not find accord with many of The Little Flock assemblies, and the movement was split. Li's followers earned the nickname, 'The Shouters' because of their practice of shouting out in their meeting en masse, 'Lord Jesus, Lord Jesus...'. In China they have been proscribed by the Communists as 'counter-revolutionary', a serious charge, and many of their leaders have been imprisoned. Some house church leaders, not connected with 'The Shouters', have been accused of belonging to them, and imprisoned.

The last of these indigenous movements was that of *The Jesus Family* which was born out of the Shandong (Shangtung) revival in the early 1930s. It was founded by a converted Buddhist, Ching Tien-ying. With the Scriptures as his only guidance Ching built up a fellowship of believers that eventually spread throughout north China and deep into the interior. They were led to structure the church so that it could function in a Communist environment. They were deeply involved in agriculture and developed most efficient land policies, which brought abundant crops.

They began to give a tenth away to the poor, and when in 1942 there was a great famine, they gave away 20% of their harvest. Before long, they were giving away nine-tenths and living on one-tenth. On forty-three acres of land they succeeded in supporting 500 people, and gave away 90% of their harvest. The Communists, who boasted of their land policies, could never compete with The Jesus Family.

Because they had no central control, would accept no foreign funds and set aside no buildings specifically for church worship the Communists could not 'nail them' on the usual charges. For this reason they were able to hold the Communists at bay when many other churches were shut down. These were policies to which they had been guided by the Holy Spirit twenty years before the Communists took over.

Born in a revival movement, where manifestations of the Spirit were normal, there was speaking in tongues, healing and casting out of demons in their meetings. In those early years they had experiences of angelic ministry and of the miraculous supply of needs.

In pointing out some of the inherent weaknesses of the missionary movement that planted the church in China, it must be remembered that those early pioneers were the spiritual children of their generation. They served God according to the light that they had received, and did so zealously. We cannot judge them according to the light God is giving his people a century and a half later.

Much that they built has withstood the wind and the flood, and together with all that has come through those indigenous and spontaneous movements of the Spirit, has found a permanent place in that building of God which is now the church in China. Without their sacrificial sowing *then* there would be no harvest *now*.

Chapter Six

THE LONG DARK NIGHT

Why do the nations rage and the peoples plot in vain? The kings of the earth take their stand and the rulers gather together against the Lord and against his Anointed One. 'Let us break their chains,' they say, 'and throw off their fetters.' The One enthroned in heaven laughs; the Lord scoffs at them. Then he rebukes them in his anger and terrifies them in his wrath, saying, 'I have installed my King on Zion, my holy hill.'

Psalm 2:1–6

There are many reasons why God chooses to visit his people with the reviving power of the Holy Spirit. One of these is to prepare them for a time of persecution. It happened in Korea before the country was torn apart by the conflict between north and south that broke out in 1950. It happened in 1953 in Zaire, or Congo as it was then known, shortly before the terrible bloodbath that followed the declaration of independence. It happened likewise in China immediately preceeding the Communist takeover in 1949.

Hundreds of missionaries who had fled the country from the Sino-Japanese war, were now returning. Significant numbers of university students were converted on the campuses and many offered themselves for full time Christian work. Despite the conflict between the Nationalists and the Communists, from many different parts there came reports of crowded churches, massive Bible conferences and successful evangelistic campaigns. Indigenous missionary societies came into being which sent missionaries to the more remote areas. The Bible Society recorded the distribution in one year of three million copies of the Scriptures. The Bible had become China's best seller.

Missionaries and other church leaders were gratified to observe that there was no looting or raping by the advancing Communist troops, nor was any immediate pressure put on the city churches. This was other than what they had been led to expect, so they pressed on with their appointed work. If some church leaders were fooled by this initial friendliness and affability of the Communists, leading evangelicals like Watchman Nee and Wang Mingdao were not. They had discerned the true nature of the Communist movement and knew that the leopard does not change its spots.

It is not difficult to see why the Communists adopted this strategy. In the first place, they did not want to antagonize Christians before they were more secure in their rulership. Then they needed the expertise of many of the Christians who were among the most capable in the community. Finally, it provided an opportunity for them to observe and take stock of the churches, and especially the leaders.

By mid-1950 the Communist rulers had set in motion a plan designed to eliminate the influence of Christianity throughout the country. Step number one was to bring the professing church under their control. They persuaded a number of Chinese church leaders to sign

Watchman Nee (1903–1972).

certain documents acknowledging that 'Christianity, consciously or unconsciously, directly or indirectly, was related to Imperialism'. It was a fact of history that Christian missions had received great benefit from western imperialist policies in China. Chinese leaders were now persuaded by Communist propaganda that the Chinese church must be totally free of western support and control. The Communist slogan, 'Love country—love church', in that order, took off.

We see here the subtlety of the Communists in making use of scriptural teaching and even Christian catch phrases, which they subverted to their own purposes. Watchman Nee was strong on the oneness of the body of Christ, that it was not to be segmented into different denominations. Some missionaries had already begun to teach that local churches should be self-governing, self-supporting and self-propagating. This became the slogan of the Communists. Their idea was to isolate the church from all outside influence, especially from the West. Once the church was united under a central organization and totally cut off from the West, it would be easy for the Party to control it. If it did not die a natural death, it could be rendered harmless.

This is the Communist thinking behind the forming of an 'official church', controlled by the State, called the Three Self Patriotic Movement. 'Patriotic' expresses the idea of 'Love country—love church', and 'Three Self' the policy of being self-governing, self-supporting and self-propagating. This party propaganda put many church leaders into a state of inner conflict. They wanted to be loyal to their country, but they had a 'gut feeling' that state control would in the long term be detrimental to the interests of the kingdom of God. It was a repeat of the crucial issue that faced those first century Christians. Who is Lord, Caesar or Christ?

Missionaries now faced the agonizing decision to stay put or pull out. The Communists did not issue an official edict, but it was abundantly clear that the new regime did not want them. The deciding question had to be, 'What is best for the Chinese church?' The Protestant societies rightly judged that their continued presence would only embarrass and hamper the Chinese believers. Accordingly they gave the order to evacuate, and by early 1952 all missionaries except the Roman Catholics had left the country.

Every branch of the Christian church now came under severe pressure. This was reflected in the sharp decline of attendances and membership in all the major denominations. By contrast, in those years from 1949 to 1957, the indigenous churches—that is, those that were not the product of western missionary activity, but had sprung up from the native soil of China—made quite dramatic gains, numbers almost tripling. Many of these were believers who were leaving their churches, now under The Three Self Patriotic movement, as they discovered the political overtones of the new organization.

The Communists then embarked on an aggressive campaign to vilify prominent leaders, especially those who were evangelical. It was not proving too difficult to bring into line denominations and para-church organizations which had central control, but the indigenous churches were proving a much more difficult proposition. In 1951 the son of the founder of The True Jesus Movement was imprisoned. The following year Jing Tianying of The Jesus Family and Watchman Nee of The Little Flock were arrested and sentenced. And in 1955 the same fate at last overtook the courageous Wang Mingdao.

Those arrested were subjected to the usual Communist brainwashing techniques. The aim was to break the will of the prisoner and compel him to submit to Marxist dogma. He needed to be re-educated. He was required to survey his past life in detail, to confess his guilt against the state, to repent and achieve a state of atonement—a perverted, and humanistic form of 'salvation'. Many stood firm through the ordeal, but others caved in.

Wang Mingdao had been a constant thorn in the side of the Communists. At first the authorities had difficulty finding a charge against him. He had refused to attend seminary, feeling it was missionary-dominated, and had never been ordained or supported financially by foreign missionaries. Like Nee, he had been fairly critical of much western missionary effort. His only education for the ministry had come from the Holy Spirit. As a man of God, the Communists could find no fault in him.

Pastor and Mrs Wang Mingdao (1984)
after more than 20 years in prison.

His church, the largest in Beijing (Peking), was always packed, and often there would be 1,000 or more outside to whom the word was relayed by loudspeaker. It could be that he preached to more Chinese than any other man. He was uncompromising over sin and proclaimed a thoroughly evangelical message. When eventually he was brought to public trial, his whole congregation was forced to attend. He was charged with being anti-government, anti-'Three Self' and preaching irregular messages. One quarter of the Christians and others present, as a result of Three-Self pressure, called for the death sentence. He was given no opportunity to speak in self-defence, but so strong was public feeling in his favour that the authorities were forced to release him.

When he was eventually brought to trial, although he never spoke against the regime, he was fearless in his criticism of the liberal clergy and the 'Three Self', whom he accused of betraying Christ. He was given a fifteen years' prison sentence. He was then subjected to the Communist re-education process. Two shifts of political experts worked on him day and night. After thirteen months of this mental torture he broke and signed a confession. This he was required to read publicly to a large audience. His capitulation made headlines on the page of every newspaper: 'I am an anti-Revolutionary criminal. I am grateful to the Government for pardoning me and saving me from the depths of my sin. . . . ' And so on.

A few days after his release he was seen walking up and down the streets of Beijing (Peking) shouting, 'I am Judas, I have betrayed my Lord.' In fact his confession did not involve a denial of Christ. A few days later, when the equilibrium of his mind was restored, he went with his wife to the government authorities and retracted his confession. 'Imprison me if you will,' he said, 'but I will not betray my Lord.' He was immediately sent back to prison together with his wife and there this courageous man of God spent the next twenty-two years, to be released in 1980 at the age of eighty.

Experiences of this kind were repeated over and over in the history of the Chinese church in Red China. Many stories will never be told. The saints who suffered were not leaders and their names never hit the headlines. They belong to the great army of God's anonymous heroes. Through the long dark night they never wavered in their loyalty to Christ. For some of them the only release they ever knew was through death to be with Christ.

The darkest phase of all was undoubtedly the Cultural Revolution. The most intensive phase of this, when the young Red Guards were in control, was 1966-69, but in fact it lasted for ten years, presided over by 'The Gang of Four'. Of course the main target of the young revolutionaries was not Christianity, or even religion in general, but 'revisionism'. Mao wanted to ensure that a new policy of liberalization would not replace the fervent revolutionary spirit that had characterized The People's Republic. So anything that savoured of the old order or the old culture was suspect.

The temples and holy places of Confucianism and Buddhism were destroyed, along with church buildings. Christianity, at least in its western form, was virtually wiped out. Even the churches of the Three-Self Patriotic Movement were forced to close down. A spiritual winter descended upon the land. In the midst of this revolution Jiang Qing, wife of Chairman Mao, and leader of The Gang of Four said, 'Christianity in China has already been put into a museum. There are no more believers.' It certainly seemed that that was the case. But in wintertime it seems that all life has taken leave of absence, although in fact beneath the surface it is being sustained and nourished, waiting to break forth with the advent of spring.

How individual Christian families fared is graphically illustrated by this account of the Luke family, told by Paul Kauffman:

> The entire family was at home when the Red Guards barged in. Two sons had graduated from a university under Communist instructors. They could not accept the Christian faith of their godly parents. Because the father had received his college education in America the entire family, including the sons, was blacklisted as undesirable by the Communists.
>
> Entering the house, the Red Guards wantonly destroyed almost everything in sight. They discovered the life-savings

which the Lukes had carefully kept for their sons' inheritance, and pocketed it. Then they demanded all Bibles and Christian books. The parents surrendered two Bibles and two copies of the book many Chinese Christians most value next to the Bible: *Streams in the Desert*. The Red Guard leader threw the books at the elder Luke saying 'Destroy these books', and with that they left.

Repulsed and disgusted by what they had seen, the two sons apologised profusely to their parents. Mr. Luke responded by saying, 'Boys, the money I had saved for your inheritance is gone, but I have something far greater to give you.' To each son he gave a Bible and a copy of *Streams in the Desert*.

Since then both boys have accepted the Lord.[5]

The long dark night for the church in China, and it is by no means over, was no accident. God was not putting his people through a survival course, to see whether they would make it. His promise holds true, 'I will build my church, and the gates of Hades will not overcome it.'[6] He was not only building his church, but using the long dark night to prepare China for what may well prove to be the greatest spiritual advance in the history of Christianity. Let us now look at how he was doing it.

Chapter Seven

CLEARING THE GROUND

*Herod and Pontius Pilate met together with the
Gentiles and the people of Israel in this city to
conspire against your holy servant Jesus .... They
did what yur power and will had decided before-
hand should happen.*

Acts 4:27–28

Jesus once described the progress of the kingdom of
heaven as 'like yeast that a woman took and mixed into
a large amount of flour until it worked all through the
dough'.[7] There is in the economy of God, a secret,
powerful spreading of the kingdom that is vividly illustrated by what was taking place in China's 'long dark
night'. When at length controls were eased and restrictions lifted, Christians from outside peered anxiously
through the bamboo curtain to see if anything had
survived. They were astounded by what began to emerge
out of the dust and rubble of the Cultural Revolution.
There was no question as to whether the Christian faith
had survived. It was alive and well and bursting forth
with new growth on every hand.

During those dark years God had not been engaged in
a mere holding operation, waiting till better days for the

advance of the church emerged. He was quietly but powerfully at work, purifying his people and clearing the ground for a new planting that he himself would accomplish. China was no virgin soil, waiting for the first tilling and sowing. More than a hundred years of missionary activity had gone before, and the situation was not without mixture and confusion. God used the Communist Revolution to perform a kind of clearing operation. This is always how God likes to work. 'I appoint you over nations and kingdoms,' he told Jeremiah, 'to uproot and tear down, to destroy and overthrow...' It sounds like a divine mandate for a cultural revolution! Then he added, 'to build and to plant.'[8]

It was God's intention to chalk up some important lessons on the Chinese blackboard for his world-wide church to ponder, but let us note first of all how he wiped the blackboard clean. In the first instance, the Communist takeover meant the removal of every missionary from China. God did not permit the removal of the missionaries because they had failed in their task. As we have already said, but for their past sowing there would be no present reaping. They had accomplished their task in the purpose of God, but it was now needful that they move on to other spheres. In this way the next phase of God's working in China could be accomplished.

We see the same principle at work in Paul, the pioneer missionary. Those New Testament missionaries never established mission stations because they were never stationary. But they did establish churches. Then often persecution drove them out and drove them on, before, as we would think, those churches were barely established.

In this the apostles were not victims either of the malice of the devil or of those who opposed them. Their steps were being ordered by the Head of the church, who saw that their exodus was essential for the growth of the young believers. The moving on of the apostles facilitated the birth of new young leadership.

There are many examples of the operation of this principle in the history of the church. In 1935 Mussolini invaded Ethiopia and Protestant missionaries were evacuated. When they returned six years later they wondered if they would find anything left of their labours. They found that the churches that they had planted had not only survived, but had grown by leaps and bounds.

In China God also used the Communists to sweep away western denominational structures. Their case against these was not so much that they were denominational as that they were western, and, in their view, the infamous tools of Imperialism. The Catholic Church with its subservience to Rome has been replaced by the Catholic Patriotic Association, headed by Marxists and totally independent of the Vatican. It is the Catholic equivalent of the Protestant Three-Self Movement.

It would be going too far to say that there is no denominationalism in China. The trappings can still be found in the open churches as well as in attitudes and practices of some of the house churches, but the old structures have gone, and in great measure the deck has been cleared.

Out of the mixture that was the Christianity of pre-Communist China God is surely preserving all that was truly the work of the Spirit. The gold, the silver and the precious stones are finding their place in the new building that he is erecting, but much of the wood, hay and stubble has been burned up in the Marxist conflagration. Like the three Hebrews in Nebuchadnezzar's burning fiery furnace, the only thing the churches have lost is their fetters, and in the flames they are finding God.

The purging work was not simply corporate—affect-

ing the church, it was inevitably individual and personal.
The Communist takeover put every professed disciple
of Christ into the crucible. None could have imagined
how hot the flames would be, or how long the ordeal.
The Lord was sitting, according to his word, 'as a
refiner and purifier of silver'. Every believer would be
tested as to the reality of his faith. The spurious would
be skimmed from the molten mixture. 'Rice Christians'
would quickly disappear from the scene. Materially
they had nothing to gain, but an awful lot to lose by a
profession of faith. Under such circumstances, who
would want to be a nominal Christian?

Even among those who were genuine believers, there
were searchings of heart and testing of motives. They
professed to love the Lord, but how much was there of
pure devotion to Christ? God had given no promise that
faithfulness to Christ would mean miraculous deliverance from persecution or even imprisonment. Had it
been so, who could be sure that his motives were pure?
'Those who are wise will instruct many, though for a
time they will fall by the sword or be burned or captured
or plundered.'[9] Even among the true believers not all
would come through the fire unscathed. 'Some of the
wise will stumble, so that they may be refined, purified
and made spotless until the time of the end'.[10]

In the Cultural Revolution the young Red Guards
made bonfires of everything that was considered a 'holy
object'. The saints had to learn as they saw Bibles,
hymn books and other Christian literature going up in
flames, that even such things as these do not constitute
the kingdom of God. The loss, painful though it might
be, would not rob them of their fellowship with Christ.

The Christian life is not even dependent upon the
possession of a Bible, however beneficial and desirable,
it is dependent on the indwelling Spirit. How vulnerable

the saints would have been down the centuries, had it been otherwise. Those first Christians of New Testament times did not possess Bibles—a complete Bible did not even exist until the close of the first century. Besides, many of the early Christians were illiterate, and could not have even benefited had they possessed a portion of the Scriptures.

Geoffrey Bull was a missionary captured by the Chinese Communists when they took possession of Tibet. During the time of his three years' incarceration they took his Bible from him. In his book, *When Iron Gates Yield* he records how God sustained him, though he deeply regretted that he had not committed more Scripture to memory. Persecuted saints down the centuries have ever proved the grace of God, even when cut off from the Bible, Christian books and the fellowship of other believers. We must all be behind every effort being made to supply Bibles to China. But this should not obscure the fact that God is demonstrating in that land that the church may still expand with remarkable rapidity, as in apostolic times, despite the absence or shortage of Bibles.

There was also a work of preparation that was being effected in the whole of Chinese society. Communism has without doubt done a great deal for China, even from the Christian point of view. The unification of the script into modern standard Chinese will greatly facilitate the rapid evangelization of the nation, as the language of common Greek had done in New Testament times. Communism has delivered the Chinese from their innate resistance to change, from crippling traditions, and has largely delivered the nation—at least as far as the younger generation are concerned—from the harmful influences of Buddhism and ancestor worship.[11]

Another great achievement of the Communists has

been in the building of roads and the supply of transport and communications. This may be linked to the Romans building their roads throughout the Empire that prepared the way for the gospel in the first century. So in China, the evangelist may now convey his message from place to place in a way that was quite impossible in pre-Communist China.

Those 'mountains' that stood in the way of the early missionary effort have in great measure been removed. Now the Communists are learning that success in destroying is one thing; ability to replace with something better is something else. Communism has promised far more than it is able to deliver.

The Cultural Revolution was a self-inflicted wound that has left a deep scar on the life of the nation. The people worshipped Mao as God, and now he lies like Dagon, flat on his face before the ark, without head or hands. Within the party there was bitter in-fighting. The heroes of yesterday have become the villains of today, and the people are left bewildered and insecure. As a result of the Cultural Revolution many urban workers lost their opportunity to better themselves through higher education, a grievous loss to most Chinese. It has left them depressed and disillusioned.

Why was President Liu Shaoqui, the man Mao had designated as his successor, toppled from power in the Cultural Revolution, disgraced and thrown into prison as 'a lackey of Imperialism'? Why, after Mao's death, was he posthumously 'rehabilitated', as the Chinese call it, and his memory honoured? It is these inexplicable swings of the political pendulum that have left the average Chinese totally bewildered. Not many are sure what is the current line, and none know when it will change.

Fox Butterfield, one time correspondent of *The New York Times* in Beijing (Peking), tells the story of a young Chinese woman called Bing. Her father was a veteran General of The People's Liberation Army who had been unjustly singled out in the Cultural Revolution and accused of being a capitalist and a traitor. Bing herself, at that time a young thirteen-year-old revolutionary, had been persuaded to testify against her father. He was sentenced to a military detention centre. After ten years in prison he was 'rehabilitated' and reconciled to his daughter. But the whole experience shattered Bing's faith in Marxism. She recounts:

> During the Cultural Revolution every household had a white plaster cast of Mao, and each day all the family members had to bow before it twice. The saying was 'In the morning ask for instructions; in the evening report back what you have done.' For those of us who survived, the Cultural Revolution was a good thing. We learned a lot. I could never put another god in my heart like Mao.[12]

For Bing, the revolutionary spirit that once possessed her had been killed stone dead; in its place—a vacuum.

Someone has summarized the post-Mao situation in these words: 'The hearts of one billion Chinese are searching for something to satisfy'—the something that Communism could not provide. This is one reason why millions are responding to the good news about Jesus.

Anyone visiting China from the West and inquiring about the Christian Church will be assured by the authorities that there is religious liberty, and will be taken, if he so desires, to one of the open churches of The Three-Self Movement to prove it. The TSPM leaders claim to speak for one united church of China. Independent house churches apparently do not exist. What is the truth?

Chapter Eight

WHICH IS THE REAL CHURCH?

*The mature...have their faculties trained by
practice to distinguish good from evil.*

Hebrews 5:14 (RSV)

It is difficult for Christians reared in democratic freedom
to understand the attitude to religion of a totalitarian
regime. We make a clear distinction between politics
and religion. To the Communist there is no difference.
His concept of 'government' is total control with no
opposition. 'Your religion,' he would tell the Christian,
'determines your way of life, your priorities, how you
spend your spare time and your money, and your attitude to government. Your religion challenges the
supremacy of the State. Of course it's political.'

In the same way Communists view their ideology as
if it were religion, atheistic though it may be. Take the
worship of Chairman Mao, and the political 'conversion'
of dissidents, involving confession of their political guilt
and indoctrination. Leading Chinese newspapers now
refer to widespread disillusionment concerning Marxism
as 'a crisis of faith'. Alexander Solzhenitsyn sums it up
perfectly: 'Where the State is sovereign, there can be no
place for any other religion.'

What the Bible has to say about this is very clear. Governing authorities have been established by God, but are therefore accountable to that higher and heavenly authority. Only God has absolute authority. 'Give to Caesar what is Caesar's, and to God what is God's.'[13] When Caesar demands what belongs to God alone, he has overstepped his heavenly mandate, and is acting without divine authority. This is the key issue now facing the church in China.

We have noted earlier how the Communists, within a few years of gaining power, tried to unite all the churches under a central umbrella, The Three-Self Patriotic Movement, and make that body in turn subject to party policy. Many Christian leaders, like Wang Mingdao and Watchman Nee, saw through this ploy from the start, and refused to co-operate. To give to the State the allegiance that belonged to the Lord alone was to them a betrayal of Christ, and they were not prepared for that, though it cost them dearly to make this stand.

Tragically, it was often—and still is—leaders and members of The Three-Self who played a leading role in the arrest, accusation and sentencing of Christians, whose only crime was their refusal to give Caesar what belonged to Christ. The attempt of the Communists to force the various branches of the professing church to become one, simply ensured that they would always be two—the open churches, subservient to the Party, and the unofficial churches that insisted, 'We must obey God rather than man.'

The distrust of Communist intentions by many Christians was more than vindicated when the Cultural Revolution overtook the nation. Even The Three-Self churches closed, and every visible form of Christianity ceased. We have seen, however, that God was in control, and working wonderfully to set the stage for a massive surge forward.

When restrictions were eased it became clear that the underground church had had an underground explosion. We mentioned earlier that before the Cultural Revolution there were about one million Protestants and three million Catholics in China. Then we began to hear of new believers being numbered, not in thousands or even hundreds of thousands, but in millions. The vast majority of these were in the house churches. This has stirred up increasing opposition from The Three-Self Patriotic Movement, whose leaders have been more active than ever in seeking to coerce the house church leaders to join The Three-Self. Where they would not co-operate, churches have been forcibly closed, and leaders arrested and interrogated.

When Three-Self representatives travel overseas they are at pains to stress that there is complete unity in the church of China, and that they are the rightful representatives and spokesmen of that church. In the West the World Council of Churches seems to have swallowed their propaganda. We must realise that leaders of the house churches have no access to the media, and when the TSPM leaders insist that they do not want Bibles and other help from the West they are *not* speaking for the silent majority of Christians in China who belong to the unofficial churches.

The Three-Self are now directing their attention to the evangelical churches, who are often in a quandary concerning what they hear about the church in China. Can they trust the statements of The Three-Self? Are these leaders truly born again? Why do so many Christians in China view them with distrust—and refuse to join them? When Christian leaders visit China they are taken to packed Three-Self churches where often sound evangelical sermons are preached, good Bible correspondence courses are available and Bibles are in plentiful supply. Is 'the official church'—its leaders hate being called this—'the real church'?

The conclusion we have to reach about The Three-Self Patriotic Movement is that it is like the curate's egg, 'good in parts'. But what does a cook do with an egg that is only 'good in parts'? Let us look at the three parts that make up the egg.

The worshippers who are undoubtedly thronging these open churches are mostly simple Bible-believing Christians, wanting baptism, the Lord's Supper, Bible teaching and the warmth of fellowship with other Christians, most of which are things which have been denied them over the past years. The fact that The Three-Self is controlled by the government doesn't really concern them. Few have any real understanding of the spiritual and political implications.

The pastors and teachers, as in the churches of the West, are a mixture. Many have been recalled from factories and communes to shepherd the flock. Some are, or have since become, born-again men who preach God's word faithfully. Others are liberal or nominal, and among these there are some that are rightly labelled 'Judases'. They denied the faith during the Cultural Revolution, and now that the situation has eased, they have climbed back on to the bandwagon. In the leadership team of an open church, one man will be a political agent, responsible to see that Party rules are kept. The born-again pastors either ignore or turn a blind eye to the political implications of belonging to The Three-Self. They do not feel that the politics of the thing is their concern. They are seizing the opportunity to preach the gospel and shepherd the flock. They say, 'The Three-Self is a good pond to fish in, so let's fish.'

The 'top brass', it would not be unfair to say, are

'political animals' rather than spiritual leaders. Often they have proved themselves more 'leftist' than Party officials, although this may be changing. As far as theology is concerned they are mainly liberals, which is no doubt the reason why the World Council of Churches is so ready to believe all that they say.

Their attitude to any evangelism may be summarized in one word, 'Don't!' The history of the first thirty years of the TSPM would suggest that there is little truth or spiritual reality in the top echelon. At the thirtieth anniversary of the movement it is reported that they prayed for the aged pastor, Wang Mingdao. Who were they trying to impress? Why did they not rather repent of their shameless betrayal of this faithful servant of God that put him and his wife behind prison bars, and robbed him of twenty-four years of public ministry? Time and again they have taken part in accusation campaigns against Christian leaders, and collaborated with the authorities in having them removed from the scene.

The Three-Self has been likened to a pyramid. The higher you get in the Movement the closer the links with the Party, and the more political you have to be. In reaching a conclusion about the TSPM churches we must not allow our minds to be confused by the fact that there are very many truly born-again Christians in its ranks. Nor that there are some devoted servants of Christ faithfully proclaiming God's word in its pulpits. We have even heard of one who uses his position to warn the house churches of any measures to be taken against them. The fact remains that the top leadership of the movement is wrong. It is political, not spiritual. It is Caesar, not Christ.

The TSPM is now the main agent of the Religious Affairs Bureau in suppressing the burgeoning house church movement. Of course they would say they are not suppressing, but seeking to bring it under control. But it amounts to much the same thing. Ding Guangxum, who heads up the TSPM, confidently asserted in 1980 that there was no division between The Three-Self churches and the House Churches. This is what he would like the world to believe. Having spoken to a Chinese brother who is regularly in touch with house church leaders right across China, I know that this is far removed from the facts of the case.

The Three-Self have their *Worship Halls*, buildings reopened for church services by permission of the Religious Affairs Bureau. These are the official 'open churches'. Then they have *Meeting Points*, which are house meetings located near the open churches, which operate under Three-Self surveillance, but have a measure of independence. The Three-Self also have registered *'Home Meetings'* which came into being after 1958, when churches were closed. Though these are free to appoint their own preachers and to manage their finances, their leaders must attend the TSPM indoctrination classes to learn about Party politics.

All these are to be distinguished from the *'Free Meetings'* of the independent house churches which have experienced such a phenomenal increase. These groups find the restrictions imposed by the TSPM wholly unacceptable. Take, as an example, these Ten Commandments put out early in the eighties by the TSPM in Henan Province.

1. Do not organize a church without the government's approval.
2. Except for government-appointed clergy, nobody should baptize.
3. Do not have contacts with foreign religious bodies

    or buy books from abroad. Violators will be prosecuted.

4. Do not print or reproduce Bibles and other religious books without approval.
5. Do not travel from commune to commune to spread religion.
6. Keep religion to yourself.
7. Do not pray every day. Pray only on Sundays.
8. Do not convey religious thoughts to persons under eighteen years of age.
9. Do not sing (religious) songs to youths under eighteen years of age.
10. Do not solicit contributions for promotion of religion, increasing believers' burdens.

Some of these injunctions may have been modified or even rescinded. But that certainly does not apply to the prohibition to influence youth. Remember, the vast majority of those in the house church movement are young people. You may be sure that a body willing to impose such restrictions on the churches in the first place, would be ready to reimpose them at any time should party policy so dictate.

The latest measure to try to control the unofficial house churches is called *The Three Designates*. It insists firstly that meetings may only be held in *designated buildings*; then, only *designated preachers* may preach at meetings or visit private homes; and finally, such preachers may not travel outside their own *designated areas* without a special permit. The designating authority in each case is the Religious Affairs Bureau.

Perhaps we are seeing in China the foreshadowing of what will be the case throughout the world before the end comes—a true church and a false church, each distinguished by its heart attitude to the lordship of

Christ. The book of Revelation shows us these two in their final expression: the Bride, 'beautifully dressed for her husband', and the Harlot, 'drunk with the blood of the saints, the blood of those who bore testimony to Jesus'. [14] Because there will be many of God's true children caught up with the Harlot, just as there are in The Three-Self in China, a voice will sound from heaven before judgement falls: 'Come out of her, my people, so that you will not share in her sins, so that you will not receive any of her plagues'. [15]

Looking at these two expressions of the church there is no need to call out, 'Let the real church in China please stand up!' It is standing up and being counted, at considerable cost.

Chapter Nine

MEET THE HOUSE CHURCH

*Greet Priscilla and Aquila, my fellow-workers
in Christ Jesus. They risked their lives for me.
Not only I but all the churches of the Gentiles are
grateful to them. Greet also the church that meets
at their house.*

Romans 16:3–4

We dismissed the taxi and made our way down a very
long narrow street, almost like an alleyway. Thankfully
there was no street lighting. The terraced shops and
apartments provided enough light just to pick our way
until we came to an unmarked doorway. A narrow
flight of wooden stairs brought us to the first floor of the
building, housing the overflow of the meeting which
was in progress. Here were Chinese Christians, Bibles
in hand and notebooks at the ready, listening to a voice
coming over the loudspeaker. Up another flight of stairs,
to a floor jammed with people of all classes. There were
professional people and students mingling with working
class people in their overalls, all sitting on simple
wooden benches.

We were conducted to the only empty seats we could
see. They had probably been reserved for us, as the

leaders knew we were coming. We found ourselves within a few feet of the preacher, whose address was being relayed throughout the house. I had read of house churches in China with 200 or more people and had often questioned how you could fit that number into a private home. Here I was, right in one. I counted over 150 people on that floor alone and even then could not see those tucked away in little rooms and cubby-holes.

This house church had four regular meetings each week, one for worship, one for prayer, one for sharing, and this was the mid-week Bible study. The house church leader who was speaking when we arrived, apart from a smile of welcome, seemed totally unaffected by our presence. The people too seemed far more pre-occupied with the message than the presence of their foreign visitors. There was a pause in the preaching, a song was announced and the people began to sing to music relayed over the P.A. system. Then the Bible teaching continued.

This house church leader, whom I would guess was about fifty, spoke the word with verve and authority. His face shone as he ministered, but it was not till afterwards I understood why. Our Chinese friend explained that he was a very courageous man of God who had spent many years in prison for his faith. He was highly respected by the other house church leaders in the area. On inquiry, we discovered that there were about 500 other house churches in this great city.

Because of the risk—not to the foreign visitors, but to their hosts, we stayed only for an hour, and then slipped away into the dark of the street. I felt that I had just for those few minutes stepped into the pages of the New Testament.

The church in the house was a significant feature of New Testament Christianity. Believers also met in caves and catacombs, or other places where much larger numbers could be accommodated. This is the situation with the so-called house churches of China. Some, particularly in the rural areas where the congregations may be quite large, have their own buildings, but most are literally churches in the house.

The church in China is demonstrating, as did the church in New Testament times, that the possession of church buildings is not at all essential for rapid growth. So often the attitude of the West is that if you haven't got a proper church building, you haven't got a proper church. But it was not until the third century after Christ that Christians were permitted to possess church buildings.

House churches in China are not a recent development. They became a distinctive feature during the early years of Communist rule. They did not come out of a reform movement that rejected traditional buildings in favour of a return to New Testament simplicity. No promoter of house churches travelled the country to spread the vision! They came out of pressure and persecution. They were born out of practical necessity. It was the best—in most cases—the only way to meet. However, behind the outward circumstances was the strategy of the Holy Spirit, providing the setting for the tremendous growth that was to come.

If this simple structure that the Chinese believers came to adopt was thoroughly New Testament, it was also distinctively Chinese. We have already noted that a strong family bond is a national characteristic, and all the efforts of the Communists to destroy this have failed. When the pressures on the Christian family became great, it was natural that the home would become a place of refuge where they could still worship, pray, read the Scriptures and encourage one another.

Some Chinese watchers see three phases of the house church movement. The first took place during the fifties as a direct result of Communist policy, and in particular because of the activities of the Three-Self Movement against Christian leaders and their churches. Those who were unwilling to worship in the Three-Self churches had no alternative but to meet in their homes. That was the first phase.

Then came the Cultural Revolution in 1966, when even the Three-Self churches closed. Those who now wished to continue to worship God had no place but the home. That was the second phase.

Then came the easing of restrictions in the post-Mao era, and with it an explosion of the house church movement. This was the beginning of phase three, and it began before the reopening of the TSPM churches. It is important to realize this, as the Three-Self like to claim that they are responsible for the resurgence of Christianity in China. When their churches did reopen, some who had left them when they closed down, drifted back, but the vast majority did not, and have not joined the Three-Self.

Because of Communist policy in the fifties, it was impossible for denominational churches to survive in their original form. Either they came under the TSPM, or they were forced to disband. At first the indigenous churches grew rapidly, and then they had to go underground. Some of these did not survive, others joined the Three-Self, while others again may still be identified among the house churches.

Many pastors, who formerly led traditional churches have become involved in the house church movement. They find house churches more intimate, more New Testament, and more Chinese in flavour than the Three-Self, with its political overtones and its formal western style services.

Not only are the Chinese family-orientated, they are community-minded. There is no character in the Chinese language for 'privacy'. The idea seems foreign to their thinking. It hit me forcibly when I walked into a crowded restaurant in Shanghai. Everywhere there were round tables with eight or ten people, and all eating out of communal dishes as they talked excitedly to one another. Sharing is natural to the Chinese. This has had a profound effect upon the spread of the gospel, leading not merely to whole families, but whole communities turning en masse to Christ.

Paul Kauffman tells of a family he knew in North China. The two daughters, who were forced to stay in China when their parents left, found their faith dulled by Marxist teaching. Yet again, it was the excesses of the Cultural Revolution that brought them back to Christ. They each witnessed to their husbands and led them to Christ. The husbands won their parents. The parents in turn witnessed to other members of the family and today, when the family meets for worship, there are nine members present.[16]

According to a recent estimate, more than half of China's one billion population are under twenty! China is a nation of young people so it is not surprising that the house churches have a preponderance of people in their twenties and thirties. Some of them are ex-Red Guards. Others are simply victims of the political vacuum that came in the wake of the Cultural Revolution. They are disillusioned by the Party's swings of policy, and by unfulfilled promises. Said a university student, 'The structure of Communism has crumbled in my mind, but I don't know what to do with the rubble.' Others are embittered because they have been compelled to sacrifice the opportunity of higher education for the cause of the Revolution.

Suddenly these disillusioned young people find themselves confronted by a revolutionary spirit of another kind. They meet committed Christians who have been purified, but not embittered by suffering, who have a joy and a holy optimism, and who witness without fear about another King and another kingdom. Thousands are finding this appeal irresistible, and whole communities are turning to Christ, Party officials and all.

Because 80% of Chinese live in rural areas, that is where most of the believers are to be found, and where the greatest advances have been seen. Since the influence of the TSPM and the location of the open churches are often confined to the cities, the rural house churches have been, to their great relief, less affected by TSPM activity. Within the cities their policy is increasingly to try to close down the house churches and compel their members to attend a newly opened TSPM church. They argue that if you don't join the TSPM you are not patriotic, but most of the house church people, who are deeply loyal to their country, do not see that loving country means loving Three-Self.

As in all indigenous movements of the Holy Spirit, these churches are strongly Bible-orientated, but that does not mean sermon-orientated. From the moment they are born into the kingdom, the young believers have a tremendous hunger for the Scriptures. This has not been dulled, but rather sharpened by a shortage of Bibles. In many cases the sole owner of a Bible in a group will tear out pages which are shared around—the community spirit again—and then laboriously copied out by hand. Reports of only one Bible amongst hundreds of believers are not uncommon in the rural areas. Like most Orientals, the Chinese have prodigious memories. Lengthy passages, even whole books, are memorized. I heard of one Christian who learned the whole of the New Testament by heart.

Some of the larger house churches, like the one we visited, are led by elderly pastors, who have been released after spending twenty years or more in prison. These stalwarts of the faith, who have come through the flames, have done a great task teaching the new Christians and in shepherding the flock.

The churches by and large are not pastor-dominated. Without realizing it, they made a practical rediscovery of 'the priesthood of all believers'. In most cases the leader will give a brief message from the Bible, and then those present will share what they have found in the passage. In some groups everyone will have copied out the relevant passage the previous week, and will come to the meeting with his or her prepared thoughts.

In pre-Communist times, Bible women who went out preaching and evangelizing in the villages did a tremendous work, especially among their women folk. Some of them are still to be found in these house churches, especially where pastors have been imprisoned, or men are not available to lead the flock. They have played a significant part in the prospering of the work, and we shall be saying something more about this later.

In country districts where Christians predominate, the churches are large and may be visited from time to time by travelling preachers. The service they perform involves outstanding courage and dedication. Beatings and imprisonment are the likely punishment should they be caught.

In a mountainous region of one of the coastal provinces there is a village with a population of 10,000, and one out of three are believers. They began to worship openly in 1976, and now there are fifteen meeting places with an average of 200 attending each place. Services are usually in the evening, from seven until eleven o'clock and consist of singing, testimony, supplication and Bible teaching from one of ten or more preachers who travel from meeting to meeting. Their messages usually last for an hour or more.

This group illustrates another important feature of these Christians, about which we shall have more to say later. They have a spirit of prayer, and they know how to exercise it. The Chinese have a saying, 'Much prayer —much power! Little prayer—little power! No prayer —no power!' Some rise at four o'clock every day to pray for their country. Those who have met with them speak of the spirit of urgency that characterizes their praying.

All over China, healing, deliverance from demonism and other supernatural manifestations of the Holy Spirit are being commonly experienced. It seems that these often flow from the fervent prayer about which we have been speaking. Like the first Christians in Jerusalem, the Chinese have cried to God to stretch forth his hand to heal, and to perform signs and wonders. We shall presently see how mightily God has answered those prayers, and what the impact of that has been upon the resultant harvest.

As well as the meetings in homes, in larger buildings or in courtyards etc., there are the outdoor meetings. These are held in parks, cemeteries or in the countryside. Sometimes they meet as though having a picnic. They sing, pray and witness. When they disperse, the church is not to be found until they meet again somewhere else. Early in the eighties this kind of meeting was common in Shanghai, but now all open-air meetings there have been banned. In the rural areas where most of the Christians are, there are very many meetings in believers' homes. As with the city house church described at the beginning of this chapter, they put aside one night for prayer, another for Bible study, another for praise etc., and often meet all day Saturday and Sunday. Where there is interference by the Public Security Bureau, the response is one of quiet resistance. But often they are so numerous that the authorities do not interfere.

The new converts are taught to evangelize others and are often in trouble for doing so. But instead of this hindering their faith it usually makes them stronger and more effective. The major work is being done by new converts who are still in their twenties. By the time they reach their thirties they are looked on as really experienced. 'Children of the Cultural Revolution are very very resourceful, experienced and dynamic.'[17]

The Christian leaders in these churches have developed instruction teams, as well as evangelistic teams. In workers' training sessions the young Christians are taught to preach. When the leaders judge them fit they are commissioned and then they join the evangelistic team. In many of these villages the one desire in the hearts of believers is to preach and build churches. Their agricultural work is simply to make a living, but most of their time is devoted to the Lord's work.

As these farming people seek first the kingdom of God, they find that 'all these things'—the necessities of life—are added to them, just as Jesus promised. The Lord blesses their crops abundantly. When others suffer from the drought, their crops thrive regardless. When other crops are spoiled by heavy rain, they have sunshine!

Evangelism is done in the evenings or during the off-season. Since 1982 the government has given back to individual house-owners much of the land that had been farmed by communes. So long as it is properly farmed, they are free to do other things. Wives and children help in the tilling of the land to enable their men to go out preaching. At harvest-time they will help each other, and then get back to their evangelistic work.

We have seen something of the characteristics and composition of these unofficial churches. Let us now look at their startling growth, and then at some of the factors that make the house church movement in China the most rapid expansion of Christianity in our day, and possibly the most rapid in the 2,000 years of the church's history.

Chapter Ten

THE SPREADING FLAME

Oh that you would rend the heavens and come down, that the mountains would tremble before you! As when fire sets twigs ablaze and causes water to boil, come down to make your name known to your enemies and cause the nations to quake before you!

Isaiah 64:1–2

As the dust and rubble began to clear in post-Mao China it was tremendously heartening to hear that behind the Bamboo Curtain the church of Christ was alive and well, and indeed, flourishing and growing. With the easing of restrictions towards the close of the seventies, Chinese Christians in Hong Kong and elsewhere were able to return to China and visit families that they had not seen for many years. It was then that the full extent of what God had been doing began to emerge. There was talk of 'millions turning to Christ', of whole communities becoming Christian, and understandably this was greeted with incredulity in many quarters. 'That can't be true!—not in Communist China!'

In a land so vast, where there were still such tight

restrictions, how could anyone be sure of these figures? Were they wild guesses, or merely spiritual optimism? Was it like some exaggerated reports one had heard in the past of 'crusade conversions'. Certainly something wonderful was happening, but what was the real extent of it?

Then more detailed reports came in from organizations whose business it was to make a careful study of the Chinese situation, and whose workers were regularly travelling to and from the mainland. They also had opportunity to question carefully those who had come out of China to Hong Kong. From many witnesses the reports one had heard began to be confirmed.

Now we have first hand accounts of the sweeping range of this great movement of the Holy Spirit. The reports are not confined to select areas or local 'bright spots', although there are vast areas still untouched. The story has been the same, from the far North, where God is at work among banished Chinese in Mongolia, to the minority tribes that dwell among the mountains of the South West; from the heavily populated coastal region, with its great cities like Beijing (Peking), Shanghai and Guangzhou (Canton), to the remote desert oasis of Xinjiang in Chinese Turkestan. House churches are known to exist in almost all of the twenty-nine provinces, with their 2,000 counties.

Despite its history of wars and political upheavals, revivals have been a recurring phenomenon in China. This has been especially the case since 1930. And even since the Revolution there have been numerous localized revivals. It is necessary here to distinguish between successful evangelism, which is the ongoing responsibility of the church, and revival, which is a thing of special times and seasons. With the one, the work, however anointed, is necessarily man-centred. With the other, there is a spontaneity that tells us God has taken the field. By this definition, not all that is happening in China can be called revival. Much of it is the fruit of God-owned evangelism and zealous witnessing on the part of the church. But the way God has moved in some areas bears the unmistakable stamp of revival.

Asian Outreach, describing what had been happening in China said:

> There was unquestionably a gracious moving of the Holy Spirit that swept millions into the kingdom of God. Soon the church, purified by the fires of persecution and open to the miracle-working power of God, had to cope with what has been described as 'the most rapid church growth in the history of Christianity'. Never before, anywhere in the world, have so many accepted Christ in such a short period of time. This was not the result of a planned evangelism programme, but rather a spontaneous move of God.

Time and again a fire from heaven has ignited the prepared twigs, and the wind of the Spirit has fanned the flames, and swept them from place to place. This is how many of the Christian leaders in China see it. A seventy-year-old pastor, who had preached one Sunday to 500 in the morning and 1,000 in the evening said, 'The fire of the gospel has been lit and it is going to keep on burning like a prairie fire.'

Let us first of all see how God is working in the far extremities of China. Over the years many in disfavour with the government, such as intellectuals, land-owners and Christians, were sent to labour camps in Mongolia. This desolate province in the far North is the 'Siberia' of China. To be sent to a labour camp there is like a death sentence. Many never return. In this bleak and inhospitable region God has been quietly but powerfully at work, as the following story reveals.

In 1980 an elderly Christian lady, one of a family of intellectuals who had been banished to Inner Mongolia, was constrained to travel by train thousands of miles south to Guangzhou (Canton). She knew no one there, but was convinced God would bring her into contact with Christians. She providentially met David Wang of Asian Outreach in the foyer of an hotel in that city, and told him how the church was mushrooming in Mongolia, with people coming to Christ in the most unlikely places and in the most unusual ways. Out of the ministry of the lady and her two sisters there are now 1,200 believers meeting in forty house churches in that desolate land.

Inner Mongolia has a population of over nineteen million, only two and a half million of whom are indigenous Mongolians. Most of the remainder are Chinese. It is amongst this latter group that God has been working. Now these in turn are reaching out to the Mongolians, who are staunch Buddhists.

Moving from the far North to the South West of China, there are minority tribes of the Miao and Lisu who are similarly responsive to the gospel. Of the 500,000 in Yunnan Province it is estimated that 50% are Christians. Among the Lisu over the border in Northern Burma the proportion is even higher, 90,000 out of 120,000. In some places entire Miao and Lisu villages have turned to Christ, and the Chinese authorities now view Christianity as the official religion of these two tribes. Often thousands of believers will gather on a mountainside to worship the Lord. As one eye-witness put it, 'Their singing ascends to the sky and hangs there like a cloud of glory.' They pray and believe with the simplicity of little children, and the Lord often honours their faith with demonstrations of signs and wonders.

Now for the provinces nearer the eastern seaboard. Open Doors recounts how a western Christian on a train met a young man who proved to be a Christian. To preserve his anonymity let's call him Tianying. He possessed a Bible that had been delivered to China by Open Doors. He had been led to Christ the previous year by his uncle, who had spent seven years in prison during the Cultural Revolution. Tianying, in turn, led his young wife to Christ in their home city in Henan Province. He said that the population of his city was about 300,000, and he believed that 100,000 professed to be Christian. Of the 6,000 in his commune, 2,000 were believers. Most of these were in their twenties and had come to Christ in the last two or three years.

His fellowship group of thirty believers met for two or three hours every Sunday night. Sometimes there was not one Bible among them. Hymn books and other Christian books were even more scarce. The meetings, he told the western Christian, consisted of singing, testimonies, prayer, thanksgiving to God and Bible reading (when a Bible was available). Occasionally an itinerant preacher would visit their fellowship to teach the word of God.

Courageous witnessing is by no means the prerogative of the grown-ups. Here is the testimony of a young man—let's call him Chiang—from Fujien Province, telling of his experience during the Cultural Revolution when he was only a teenager. While she was in hospital, a Christian sister from his house church was able to share the gospel with the woman in the next bed, who had been a fervent idol worshipper all her life. Later, on her discharge from hospital, Christians in the house church led her and her daughter to the Lord.

The one big fear of the mother was her husband. He was a huge and violent man, and a staunch Communist cadre.[18] He was shortly due to be coming home from the country where he was in charge of a commune and labour camp. How could she dare let him know that she had become a Christian? As it was, every day he lost his temper and got mad at her. This might be too much.

The Christians prayed fervently, and the Communist cadre was invited to visit brother Chiang's family, as his wife had told him how kind they had been to her in hospital. In the heart of the young fifteen-year-old boy the word of God was like a fire. He knew he had to tell this man, who could well drag them all off to prison, that they were Christians. Out came the truth. The man, angry and red in the face, told the lad that this was nothing but superstitious nonsense. Amazingly, the mixture of abuse and Marxist rhetoric did not extinguish the fire of the lad's zeal. He found himself answering the big man to his very face. God's word was indeed a fire and the truths of creation, sin and judgement were laid bare.

The hardened cadre was left dazed and speechless. As he saw his sin and God's awesome holiness he began to tremble. The impossible was happening. There, in Chiang's humble Christian home, the visitor, with great tears of repentance, found the Saviour. His wife recently wrote to Chiang telling him that ever since that day her husband had not once lost his temper, and that they daily read the Bible, sang and prayed together.[19]

A worker in Asian Outreach tells of what happened to a western missionary on a train journey in China. At a scheduled stop a young hawker entered the compartment. Trying to make conversation with the foreigner, he said in his very broken English, 'I am Christian. You Christian?' With his fluent Mandarin, the missionary could have eased things for this young man, but he coolly replied in English, 'Yes, I am a Christian.'

Perhaps the young man had gleaned that most westerners like to think that they are Christian because they belong to a so-called Christian country. Anyway, he wasn't satisfied, and pressed the point: 'Are you a two-time born Christian?' Still the missionary held back and asked this young man to explain. He was turning red with excitement as he tried so hard to get this uninformed white fellow to understand what the new birth was all about.

At length the missionary took pity, and told him that he spoke Chinese. The young man's face shone, as he began to explain in his native tongue what it means to be a true Christian. The missionary was amazed both at his enthusiasm and his sense of urgency. 'You must become two-time born Christian!' he urged. At length the missionary explained that he was both born again and a missionary.

'Good!' proclaimed the young hawker, 'how many did you bring to Christ last month?'

The story did not reveal how the missionary responded to that 'fast ball', but he discovered that this young man had been in training for The People's Liberation Army when he was converted and compelled to leave. Returning to his village, he joined a rapidly growing fellowship. When they saw he had the gift of evangelism they helped him to get a licence so that he could sell on the trains. 'I love to tell everyone about Jesus,' he said. 'We must work while we have opportunity, because Jesus is coming back soon.'

Proof of the manner in which this work of God is spreading is supplied when Christians from outside revisit a place only to find that the tally of believers has multiplied incredibly. At the end of 1979 workers from Asian Outreach visited a village, part of a large commune, in Xinjiang Province. There were few Christians in that village, they were told. Six months later, they returned, to be told, 'Now there are few unbelievers in the village!' Since then there has been a spiritual awakening in the whole area, and the visitors were told, 'This is now a Christian Commune, and there are very many such in this Province.'

Paul Kauffman tells of his interview with a young man of twenty-eight who came across to Hong Kong. As a schoolboy he had, like so many, rejected the faith of his parents, and accepted the philosophy of Marxism. Through the witness of a friend, he yielded his life to Christ, was baptized and became part of the house church. In his home city with a population of 400,000, he reckoned there were 50,000 Christians. That works out at one in eight. Only one pastor had come through the Revolution. He was over eighty, but had an active ministry of Bible teaching and counselling.[20]

A remarkable feature of this movement is the way God uses the elderly who are now free after years in prison. Many are retired, so are free to travel and don't need to earn their livelihood. They are the backbone of the leadership of the house churches. Aged pastors experience unbounded joy as they teach and preach again and see the response of the young people to their ministry. One ninety-year-old pastor returned to his village in South China and a church of 700 members sprang up there in just three months! Another similarly built up a church of 400 members in West China.

Amazing is the story of what God has done in a provincial capital of the East coast. By 1973 there was a Christian community of over 1,000. The authorities beame alarmed and ordered the meetings to cease. The following year five leaders were arrested, paraded in dunce's caps and imprisoned. On release they continued their pastoral ministry, and the numbers of believers increased dramatically.

In this same city, a Chinese bishop, whose predecessor had been tortured to death in 1980, reported that believers in the city numbered 2,000. Further afield, in seven remote mountain villages he had visited in the course of his pastoral ministry, he found 7,000 new Christians, being taught by two elderly workers. By 1980 Christians throughout the Province were known to number 600,000. In one area in a single year 6,000 new believers were baptized. Christians were beginning to appear even in Communist Party ranks and in the Youth League.

Still more remarkable is what God is doing in many of the communes. This report comes from the coastal province of Zhejiang. There is one commune of 10,000 which is totally Christian. The officials have named the production teams 'Jesus Team Number One, Jesus Team Number Two' etc, and they have been held up as an example to other communes because of their consistently high production levels.

One could describe what is happening in many parts of China as 'group conversion'. It usually comes about when there is a powerful working of the Holy Spirit in a group or community. It begins with the conversion to Christ of a recognized leader or a number of leaders. This produces a chain reaction, and the group turns en masse to Christ. It is not a psychological phenomenon, or a case of the pack slavishly following the leader. Each one must respond personally. That is why some prefer the expression 'multi-individual' conversion rather than 'group conversion'. It is just that God uses one decision to trigger off another.

The strong family ties and the strong sense of community among the Chinese make this a likely event, especially when the Spirit of God is moving powerfully.

Of course this has worked both ways. It was those very family and community relationships in the Pre-Revolution era that made the task of evangelism so difficult for the missionary.

The inland province of Henan (Honan) has witnessed this incredible 'people movement'. With a population of seventy million, 'astounding numbers have been turning to the Lord, whole villages or production teams at a time'. In one county it is estimated that the Christians number 300,000 out of a population of 700,000 and they are actively supporting and participating in witness teams who are spreading the gospel.

Leslie Lyall, an expert on China, and a former missionary to that land, records, 'In some rural areas over 90% of the population are Christian'—and this he describes 'as a totally unprecedented statistic in the history of the church in China'. It is probably unprecedented in the history of the church anywhere.

None have been more used in spreading the flame in China than the itinerant preachers. None have paid a heavier price in the fulfilment of their calling. Before we look at other means that God has been using, let us hear the challenging words of one preacher, who has been 'tramping for Jesus' since the sixties. Somehow he has avoided arrest, although many times he has had narrow escapes. He says:

> Although I give very little, the Lord receives my service. The Lord continues to train me and lead me in the revival work as he puts me among believers all over the land. Thank the Lord for his mercy.
>
> The Lord does not give us worry-filled hearts; rather our hearts are filled with peace and consolation. The Lord loves us, so what can people do to us? He whom we trust gives us strength so that we can do all this. Thank the Lord for his grace. We know we must obey our Lord, not

men, because he gives us his precious power and faith. When we go preaching from village to village the Lord gives us these words to console us. We know that those who trust in him will be rich and blessed. We praise and thank the Lord that now the powerful fire of his revival is spreading. The miracles of his power extend to all the lands. The faith in the hearts of the itinerant preachers brings that fire to all places, and then the fire spreads from one place to the next, from one province to another.[21]

This account could not be complete without special mention of the outstanding part that women have played in 'spreading the flame'. Back in the early missionary days, many Chinese women trained in Christian schools and local churches, dedicated their lives to Christ's service, and became known as 'Bible Women'. In those days women in China were very secluded and did not attend public meetings. It was the Bible Women, alongside the lady missionary, who reached them in their homes—visiting the sick, teaching hygiene and child care, and befriending these 'inside persons'. Later, when such women began attending church, the Bible Women would teach them to read and write, for most were illiterate. They would also be involved in village evangelism.

During the first thirty years under the Communist regime, when so many pastors, evangelists and leaders were in prison, it was primarily the Bible Women, though no longer called by that name, who stepped into the breach and kept the churches together. Where a Barak is unwilling or not available for the task, God does not hesitate to raise up a Deborah. There are 'aged Deborahs' still feeding flourishing churches in China, as in the case of the ninety-year-old who has a congregation of over 500 believers. Another wrote to Marjorie Baker, a former missionary to China, 'I made a trip to the villages once every two months last year to preach the gospel. God worked in people's hearts and many were saved. A blind man and a mentally-ill person were healed.'

There is now a whole new generation of young people in the house churches who have grown up under Communism. The willingness of the young women among them to suffer for Christ has not been one whit less than that of the young men. Hua Ling, as we will call her, is now twenty-one. She was born in a village in Central China. When eleven, she came across a hand-copied booklet that told the way of salvation. In child-like faith she trusted in Christ. She never met another Christian, nor did she have a Bible, but she read and re-read the little booklet. How she longed to share the Good News with others. When there came some political relaxation in 1980, she witnessed to her mother and some neighbours, and they were converted.

Hua Ling realized that God had given her the gift of evangelism. He continued to bless her ministry and brought her in touch with other Christians. They shared testimonies and worship, and built each other up. The message of the gospel spread, and many came to believe. Seeing the fields white for harvest Hua Ling decided to become a full-time evangelist. Not fearing reproach, she gave up her job and went with others to spread the gospel in neighbouring villages. Everywhere she went, people turned to Christ. Revival came to the villages and Christians were renewed in their faith.

A retreat for young people, from eighteen to forty years old, was organized at the time of the Spring Festival, and 190 attended. The theme was 'The Needs of the Harvest Field'. Many present wept before the Lord and expressed willingness to give up their jobs and give themselves to evangelism. The leaders selected those they felt were called of God.

Hua Ling and her colleagues have experienced suffering and persecution both in the towns and the countryside. They have been beaten, kicked and stunned by electric shocks. Three of the brothers in their party were arrested and detained. Far from being frightened, they rejoiced to be counted worthy to suffer for Christ.[22]

God has also greatly used the radio in spreading the flame. They say that all of China listens to the radio. China travellers report that they can pick up clear Christian broadcasts, even in the farthest corners of the country. They continually meet those who testify to finding Christ through the radio broadcasts. Pastors and leaders eagerly devour the programmes specially designed to help them in their ministry. Countless Christians tune in regularly for spiritual food. A Christian leader in Hong Kong reported to me that the believers on the mainland tell him, 'We don't want classical music (between programmes). The time is too precious. Use it for preaching the gospel, or for feeding us Christians!'

It is almost impossible to comprehend a movement so vast in its scope and so rapid in its multiplication. Inevitably we begin to ask questions. What are the causes of this unprecedented move of God? Are there some 'success secrets' here that we can learn and apply? It needs to be said at once that the ways of God can never be reduced to a spiritual formula. They are not as simple as that. In the first place there is always a mystery element—inexplicable factors bound up with the will of God and the timing of God. We have to remember that God always reserves the right to do 'as he pleases with the powers of heaven and the peoples of the earth',[23] and he is under no obligation to 'give account of all his doings'.[24]

Nevertheless there are vital lessons for us to learn. So before we enquire, 'What can we do to help the church in China?' it may be more appropriate—and certainly more humbling—to ask the question, 'What has the church in China to teach us?' Without doubt God is chalking up many things on the China blackboard that he wants us to learn. We may find that not all are lessons we are eager to embrace. As this book now moves from the China story to considering the spiritual lessons, let us ask God to give us humble, teachable and willing hearts.

PART TWO

The Church in China Speaks

Chapter Eleven

BLOOD RED SOIL

In truth, in very truth I tell you, a grain of wheat remains a solitary grain unless it falls into the ground and dies; but if it dies, it bears a rich harvest.

John 12:24 (NEB)

Many years ago some tourists were visiting the Colosseum, Vespasian's famous amphitheatre in Rome. 'Take a handful of the soil,' said the guide, 'it's all martyrs'.' I recall the sense of awe that came upon me when I too gazed on that same great arena when visiting Rome as a soldier. This was the spot where Nero let loose the lions on Christians for the entertainment of the lords and ladies of Rome. Their crime? They had confessed, 'Christ, not Caesar, is Lord.' Nero and the pomp of ancient Rome have passed away, but the kingdom for which those early Christians suffered and died marches on in triumph.

Those were the crude and cruel days of the first century, we may think, but surely our advancing civilization has changed all that? May we not now accomplish the triumph of the kingdom without blood and tears? The words of Jesus at the head of this chapter may be familiar to us. We may see them fulfilled in the cross of Christ. Was he not that grain of wheat that fell into the ground and died? Are we not the harvest? True, but not the whole truth. We cannot bury the cross in the great historic past, and assume that this 'life-out-of-death' principle that Jesus was talking about was totally fulfilled at Calvary. He himself taught that every disciple must take up the cross and carry it with him. The church in China will tell you, that for them, the cross is very much a present experience, though worked out in a variety of ways.

Here surely is the primary reason why this work of the Holy Spirit in China is more swift, spontaneous and powerful than anything we generally experience here. These believers have a totally different attitude to suffering, hardship and persecution than Christians in the West. To us, these may be the unfortunate and occasional 'accidents' of the Christian life, to be avoided if at all possible. When they do occur we probably view them as dastardly attacks of Satan to be stoutly resisted in the name of the Lord, and we trust for speedy deliverance from them. Let us test this attitude by the consistent teaching of the New Testament.

From the outset of his ministry Jesus warned his disciples to be ready for persecution. He did not wait until they were all fully mature and wholly sanctified before he introduced them to this 'nasty' side of the Christian life. One reason for this is that persecution and suffering has a very real part to play in that very maturing and sanctifying process. In his first discipling course Jesus said, 'Blessed are those who are persecuted because of righteousness', and he gave no hint that this 'dubious blessing' would pass away as the gospel triumphed in this age.

Jesus then went on to stress the importance of this beatitude by amplifying it in a way that he did not do with any of the others. He continued, 'Blessed are you when people insult you, persecute you and falsely say all kinds of evil against you because of me. Rejoice and be glad, because great is your reward in heaven, for in the same way they persecuted the prophets who were before you.'[25] That's heavy stuff for new converts!

When Jesus himself came to face the cross, he never faltered. 'Now my heart is troubled,' he confessed, 'and what shall I say? "Father, save me from this hour"? No, it was for this very reason I came to this hour. Father, glorify your name!'[26] Jesus never looked for a way *out*, he only looked for a way *through*—that he might glorify the Father in the path of suffering.

That little band of disciples was evidently not demoralized by what Jesus had said and by what he later experienced. Following Pentecost they began to witness as Jesus had commanded them in the power of the Holy Spirit. The opposition that Jesus had predicted was not long in coming. After being flogged and then ordered not to speak in the name of Jesus, 'The apostles left the Sanhedrin, rejoicing because they had been counted worthy of suffering disgrace for the Name.'[27]

Paul's initiation into the Christian faith was no different from that of his fellow apostles. From the time of his conversion on the road to Damascus the Lord began to 'show him how much he must suffer'[28] for his sake. Paul in turn encouraged his new converts, 'to remain true to the faith', warning them, 'We must go through many hardships to enter the kingdom of God.'[29]

A little later he wrote to the church in Philippi. He exhorted them to conduct themselves in a manner worthy of the gospel of Christ, and not to be frightened by the opposition. Then he informed them, 'For it has been granted to you on behalf of Christ not only to believe on him, but also to suffer for him.'[30] Has anyone

—beside Paul—ever told us that, alongside the privilege of *believing in Christ*, we have been accorded the privilege of *suffering for Christ?*

Paul saw the dynamic of this principle as the secret of the incredible effectiveness and abiding fruitfulness of his own ministry, and that of his fellow workers. He explained it this way:

> We have this treasure in jars of clay to show that this all-surpassing power is from God and not from us. We are hard pressed on every side, but not crushed; perplexed, but not in despair; persecuted, but not abandoned; struck down, but not destroyed. We always carry around in our body the death of Jesus, so that the life of Jesus may also be revealed in our body. For we who are alive are always being given over to death for Jesus' sake, so that his life may be revealed in our mortal body. So that death is at work in us, but life is at work in you.[31]

Without any shadow of doubt this unparalleled harvest that is being reaped in China is directly related to the way the church there has willingly embraced the way of the cross, and continues to do so. 'A grain of wheat,' said Jesus 'remains a solitary grain unless it falls into the ground and dies; but if it dies, it bears a rich harvest.' For China this is not a feature peculiar to the late twentieth century. It has been true there since the church was planted. Many indeed are the grains that have fallen into the ground and died. See how great the harvest! In the words of Samuel Zwemer,

> There is no gain without a loss,
> You cannot save without a cross.
> The corn of wheat to multiply
> Must fall into the ground and die.
> Whenever you ripe fields behold,

Waving to God their sheaves of gold
Be sure some corn of wheat has died,
Some saintly soul was crucified,
Someone has wrestled, wept and prayed,
And fought hell's legions undismayed.

It began with those pioneer missionaries. It is all too easy for us, living in the comfortable affluence of the twentieth century, to be armchair critics of that early missionary movement. They made mistakes, and it would be foolish of us not to learn from them. But when it comes to hardship, suffering and sacrifice, we have to sit at their feet. Speaking of his pioneer evangelism, Paul once said, 'I do not consider my life of any account as dear to myself, in order that I may finish my course, and the ministry which I received from the Lord Jesus.'[32] Those pioneer missionaries to China may not have understood much about apostolic ministry but they certainly possessed this apostolic spirit.

The call of Christ to China meant a five month voyage, cooped up in some cargo ship, before they even saw the people to whom they had been called. Then they found themselves strangers in a strange land coping with a different climate, different diet, a different culture, and with many months of hard graft grappling with a strange language. All this before they could even make themselves understood. Then for many there were the hardships of pioneering the gospel among a people that were initially suspicious, prejudiced and unresponsive.

There were no jets to whisk them away to the homeland and give them a furlough break every year or two. Some of them never saw their homeland again. Outbreaks of violence like the Boxer Rising took their toll. Young parents sometimes faced the agony of little ones struck down with fatal diseases, and then tearfully laid to rest in the soil of China. But for almost all, hardships, suffering and self-denial were the order of the day. Like Paul they knew what it was to die daily. 'We *always* carry around in our body the death of Jesus…are *always* being given over to death for Jesus' sake.' Day by day the price of the harvest was being paid, as seeds fell into the ground and died.

For some there was immediate return, but many never saw a full harvest. If they were alive, they would see it now. As a servant of God once said to me, 'If you suffer without reaping, it is that others may reap after you. And if you reap without suffering, it is because others have suffered before you.' Both suffering and reaping are for ever joined in the economy of heaven.

Though we understand in the natural realm that the grain of wheat has to die before the harvest can come, we may wonder why this has to be true in the spiritual realm? In the first place, suffering is a means of purifying. It is like a threshing instrument. None of us likes being 'threshed', but how else is the chaff in our lives to be separated from the grain? None of us relishes being subjected to the flame, but how else is the dross to be separated from the gold? A pure church is a powerful church, one through which the Spirit may flow unhindered.

There is a sense in which the cross comes to cleanse the church from racial and cultural impurities. This has happened in China, as Carl Lawrence has vividly expressed:

Slowly, surely, we can hear the quiet procession of the shuffling feet, from every part of China, as they made their way to a hillside; there was the sound of someone digging, and then the thump of a cross being set upright; the pounding of nails, and slowly, old superstitions, ancestral worship, arrogance of being a superior race, bitterness for feeling they have been forgotten, ambitions, desires, security, creature comforts; the hills of China were alive with hundreds of years of history hanging from crosses. A twentieth century Nero helped purify Christ's church.[33]

Then, as we saw earlier in this book, God has used the Communist Revolution in great measure to purify 'a fragmented denominational church which reflected all the idiosyncrasies of western individualism', to be a suitable instrument in the hands of the Holy Spirit.

Hence the history of the church in China since 1949 has been a history of suffering. Yet by going through different stages of suffering, the church in China has been transformed from a timid, foreign-coloured institutional church into a bold, indigenous institutionless church, and it has been changed from a dependent mission church to an independent missionary church. It is a church that has gone through the steps of the cross, following the footsteps of her Lord: betrayal, trial, humiliation, abandonment, suffering, death, burial, resurrection, and the gift of Pentecost...Christians in China interpret the last 34 years of prolonged suffering as a gift of God's profound grace to the Chinese church to cleanse her from her impurities, to test the genuineness of her faith and loyalty, to train her for obedience and progress unto greater maturity, and to enable her to gain a deeper experience of Christ.[34]

It has been said that 'the Chinese church has from the beginning been a martyr church', but never a church with a martyr spirit. It is not eaten up with self-pity because of its hard lot, but is joyful and triumphant.

Again and again it has been the consistent joy of believers that has been the powerful magnet which attracted their fellow Chinese to a forbidden faith. Take this eye-witness account of believers being driven away to prison:

> The people of the street could not see the people inside the cart, but they thought that they were awful criminals to be dragged away like animals. The authorities did not want us to see them. 'Are they really that sinful?' we asked. Then we found out the truth. These were Christians on their way to jail. They were all handcuffed together and they were happy. There was no dissatisfaction or resentment on their faces. We could hear them singing as they went by, 'Lord, you are worthy to receive praise. Praise the Lord.'

Or take this story of a sister who spent twenty-four years in prison:

> She was in prayer when the authorities arrived to arrest her. She was not surprised, as the Lord had already prepared her heart. In fact, just as they arrested her, the Holy Spirit came and filled her with an uncontainable joy. As the car in which she was being taken away jostled down the road, she was overflowing with joy and sang all the way. The authorities naturally suspected that she was demented.
>
> As she was being registered at the prison she had time to witness at length to one of the officials. So powerful was her anointed witness that right then and there he accepted Christ. As he registered her she said to him, 'Today is not the day I came to register myself, and I will never really be a prisoner here—Christ will constantly be with me. I am free. This is the day when you have registered your residency in the kingdom of God.'
>
> Some time later, all the inmates were given an envelope containing the length of their sentence. The other inmates asked her how long her sentence was. She answered, 'I don't know. I just put the edict away without looking at it.'
>
> 'Why?' they asked. 'Don't you want to know how many years you are getting?'

'It doesn't matter,' she replied. 'Whether it is ten years or one hundred years, each day will be a day with my Lord.'

In one prison they were inhumanely crowded—ten prisoners to a tiny cubicle. They were not allowed to speak to each other or doze off during the day. A guard periodically looked into the room through a glass opening in the door. Many fell ill—others lost their minds. One prisoner whispered to her, 'We can see that your religious faith really gives you strength.'

Another day the guard burst into the room and shouted at her, 'Stop your smiling.'

'I am not smiling,' she replied.

'Yes, you are,' shouted the guard.

When he left, the other prisoners said, 'Your eyes are always smiling and your face glows with joy, even when you are not smiling.' Most of her fellow prisoners were not Christians—that is, they were not Christians until she led numbers of them to the Lord.

The word *martyr* is the Greek word for a 'witness'. That suggests to us that from the earliest times a martyr church and a witnessing church were one and the same. That is certainly true in China, as this story told by David Wang reveals:

Martha was 18, young in both age and in Christian experience, when I first met her in central China. She had become a Christian through listening to our radio broadcasts. She corresponded with us in Hong Kong and we nurtured her. Two years later I had the opportunity to meet this young Chinese girl again. She was working in a factory, but she urged us to let her do something for the Lord. She did not want money, or a bicycle. What she wanted was to be regularly supplied with Bibles, so that she could distribute them to the remotest provinces of China.

Martha was never on our payroll. But, from time to time, we helped to cover her travelling expenses. She was travelling and ministering, looking to God to meet her needs. I recall meeting her once in the city of Xian in 1981. We had arranged to meet at 9 p.m., but she did not turn up until about 1 a.m. She had been delivering Bibles in a nearby village when the local commune leaders discovered what she was doing. They beat her up, robbed her, and threw her on to a deserted road. It was only a miracle that she was able to hitch-hike to our rendezvous.

Even in the darkness of the park, I noticed that something was wrong with Martha. Her head was swollen like a basketball.

'What is the matter with you?' I asked. 'Did they beat you up like this?'

'Oh no,' she said, 'I've had this problem for nearly two months now.' Then she rolled up her pants to show me legs covered with stings and mosquito bites. 'I think it's some kind of blood poisoning.' As she travelled in the remote countryside of China, often she had to sleep in deserted huts and derelict temples. She was being literally 'beaten up' by bugs and mosquitoes.

'Tomorrow we must go to a doctor,' I urged her. 'No, no,' she said. 'I have to catch an early train tomorrow to go to Inner Mongolia. Where are the Bibles?' Her only concern was to get the Bibles to Inner Mongolia.

Two years later, in August 1983, we suddenly lost contact with Martha. There was no news from her or about her for a long time. It was the time of China's 'Anti-Crime Campaign'. Many people were arrested and executed throughout China. We became quite concerned for Martha.

Later we got a letter from her through her friends. It was not really a letter, just a little piece of paper. She had been arrested and charged with distributing 'superstitious materials' in the People's Republic of China. The little note read: 'I don't know what the penalty will be, but please'—quoting Paul's words—'Pray for me that whenever I open my mouth, words may be given me so that I will fearlessly make known the mystery of the gospel, for which I am an ambassador in chains.' A few weeks later, we received news that 24-year-old Martha was 'with Christ'. She had been executed.

Yes, the soil of China has been made rich by the blood of its martyrs.

> O cross, that liftest up my head,
> I dare not ask to fly from thee,
> I lay in dust life's glory dead,
> And from the ground there blossoms red
> Life that shall endless be.
>
> *(George Matheson)*

*Tiananmen Square – Gate of Heavenly Peace.
Beijing (Peking).*

Chapter Twelve

BY THIS THEY CONQUER

They have conquered him [Satan] by the blood of the Lamb and by the word of their testimony, for they loved not their lives even unto death.

Revelation 12:11 (RSV)

The progress of the kingdom in China is, in so many ways, strikingly similar to what we find in the New Testament. It advances in the teeth of relentless opposition, and it is being paid for in blood.

Paul tells us that the reception of the gospel by those in Thessalonica was with 'severe suffering' and yet with a joy inspired by the Holy Spirit. From their conversion these believers were aggressive in their witness to Christ. Paul told them that they were a 'model' to the churches throughout the whole of Greece.[35] They are surely a model to the churches of all time.

This is how it is in China. God has lit a flame in the hearts of thousands of Chinese believers that is a challenge and a rebuke to the easy-going Christianity in the West. As with the epic story of Elijah on Mount Carmel, the authorities have poured their barrels of water on the sacrifice, and the fire of God has come, not only consuming the sacrifice, but even licking up the water in the trench.[36]

In its evangelism, the house churches of China do not seem to put any stress on the diplomatic approach, or on waiting for what we like to call 'the God-given opportunity'. No doubt there is a place and time for this. But in China, God is on the move, and the saints are moving with him. Itinerant preachers, as we have seen, go from village to village, and from county to county, proclaiming the good news, often to quite large gatherings. Locally, the believers who have been trained in evangelism are organized into teams, and go forth to witness to all who will listen. They all know the penalties for breaking the rules—arrest and interrogation, beatings and imprisonments—but none of these things deter them.

A report late in 1983 speaks of the arrest of nineteen church leaders in one county in the North of China, and eighty others who were forced to flee from their homes because of the threat of arrest. As the more seasoned pastors are arrested, or are forced to flee, a new generation of leaders is taking their place.

Younger men and women are also taking over some of the itineraries of the older preachers, who are now in prison or in self-exile. In the face of restrictions, they travel circuits and many villages, preaching and counselling daily. They keep exhausting schedules, often travelling fifty to sixty miles a day by foot, and ministering late into the night.

Christians see the hand of God even in this persecution, for those in prison are now able to sleep regularly for the first time in many months. Those who have fled their homes have gone into other provinces where they continue to spread the Gospel.[37]

A group of house church leaders met in Central China. Their major concern was the growing opposition of the Three-Self Patriotic Movement to any evangelistic outreach. They were determined to reach out for Christ in spite of it. Here is the gist of the seven point resolution that they adopted, and circulated in their churches:

1. Let the message of the cross be spread wherever we go. We must make every believer know clearly that he is saved by the blood of the Lamb.

2. Our situation is a precarious one. We are under heavy pressure, and many brothers and sisters are being arrested by local authorities. Our meetings are being stormed and dispersed. Our Bibles are taken away, so we see clearly that we have to tread the path of the cross. We must have a willingness to suffer for Christ.

3. Many believers are still very confused as to the real design of the Three-Self Patriotic Movement, and its power is getting stronger every day. In a way it is good to have the TSPM open churches in the cities so that believers can have places for worship. But for us in the villages, the setting up of the TSPM meeting points (house churches) is a trap. Those who fall into that trap can no longer serve the Lord according to the leading of the Holy Spirit. The TSPM forbids itinerant preachers to preach the gospel in places where it is most needed. The TSPM also forbids Christian workers from different places having fellowship with each other, thus we can no longer hold larger meetings. But we are able to hold smaller meetings of eighty to a hundred people at night. We have to meet in different homes each night, just as we used to before 1976. But God is blessing house church meetings, and is opening wide for us doors which no one can close.

4. We are to build the church on the foundation of Jesus Christ. We are called to be builders of his

church. So we must teach the people what the church of Christ really is. All our work must be arranged according to the Biblical teachings of the church, and we must make Christ the centre of our life's work.

5. We are stepping up fellowship among Christian workers so that we are linked together in love, and together we will work towards a general goal of evangelism of China.

6. To strengthen the church we must have the life of Christ to supply that life to other new members. We must train more young workers so that they can shepherd the new converts and let them grow in their life in Christ.

7. This is the idea of preaching the gospel as we tread the land, claiming the land for Christ's kingdom. Wherever we go, we preach Christ. Whoever we meet, we shall win them for Christ, so that they shall also join us. We shall send preaching teams to mountainous and faraway places where the gospel has not yet reached. We are already able to lead people in village after village to turn away from idols to Christ. They then burn up their idols after repentance and faith in Christ.

Such is the indomitable spirit among the leadership of the house churches in the face of the opposition of the Three-Self and the Communist authorities.

It is important to understand the nature of persecution and what its real object is. Just as certainly as the church's conflict is not against flesh and blood, whether Communist or other, so persecution is not aimed at the church, but at Jesus. When Saul of Tarsus was breathing out threatenings and slaughter against the disciples of the Lord, Christ called to him 'Saul, Saul, why do you persecute me?' Persecuting the church is really persecuting Christ. There are churches, even under Marxist regimes, which are not being persecuted. There is so little true manifestation of the life of Jesus. But where the life of Jesus is very active, persecution is a present reality. Spiritual vigour among the people of God demands the close attention of the Devil. There are many Christians whom the Devil can well afford to leave alone because they are no danger to him.

Early in 1985 I asked a pastor in Hong Kong who was constantly in and out of China, whether the great wave of blessing in the early eighties was being maintained. He replied that it was continuing, but that it had slowed down in many areas due to persecution. He felt that it was a good thing that the mass growth of a few years back had given way to a time of separation of the true from the false, and a time of consolidation. 'The God of all grace...after you have suffered a little while, will himself restore you and make you strong, firm and steadfast.'[38]

This issue of suffering for Christ is the big test of where a believer's heart really is. If it is down here, the prospect of some heavenly reward 'in the sweet by-and-by' has no big appeal. He wants instant deliverance from 'the nasty now-and-now'! But if heaven has really captured his heart, if earthly things have faded in the light of eternal realities, his attitude to suffering radically changes. He finds he is able not only to rejoice, but even 'leap for joy' as Jesus taught. The attitude to suffering is crucial. If believers have not come into victory here, hard times bring witnessing to a halt.

Apart from the purifying and maturing of the church through suffering, it seems in some inexplicable way to release the power of God, often with electrifying effect. The principle of the cross at work in a yielded life can crack opposition, melt the hardened heart and open a tightly shut mind to the light of truth. This has been demonstrated again and again in China.

A letter from Henan (Honan) Province written in 1982, tells of ten young people who, after earnest prayer, set out to preach. As they proclaimed the gospel with tears, passers-by stopped to listen, fortune-tellers (of whom there are many in China) broke down and wept, and workers on their way home from the factories forgot their hunger and stayed to listen as God's power was present. The large crowd would not let them stop, tired though they were. Then came the Public Security Bureau officials, who tied up the young preachers, dragged them away and beat them until they were unconscious.

In the party was one girl who was only fourteen. When, after being thus beaten, she revived and continued witnessing, all kinds of people broke down, repented and believed in Jesus. It was similar with four of the young men in the party. They were forced to kneel for three days without food or water. Even as they were being beaten until the blood flowed, they continued praying, singing and praising the Lord, until even their tormentors were converted and believed the gospel. They could have looked their officials in the face and boldly delcared, 'Death is at work in us, but life is at work in you.'[39]

The report concludes:

So in this area recently, the flame of the Gospel has spread everywhere. There has never been a revival here before, but through the persecution, this place has truly the seeds of life. May everyone who hears of this give thanks and praise for the revival of the church in this area. In men's eyes, this is an unfortunate happening, but for Christians it is like a rich banquet. This lesson cannot be learned from books, and this sweetness is not usually tasted by

men. This rich life does not exist in a comfortable environment. Where there is no Cross there is no crown. If the
spices are not refined to become oil, the fragrance of the
perfume cannot flow forth, and if grapes are not crushed in
the vat, they will not become wine.

Dear brethren, these saints who have gone down into
the furnace, far from being harmed, have had their faces
glorified and their spirits filled with power, with greater
authority to preach the Word and a far more abundant
life. The Lord will have the final victory in their bodies,
making Satan to be ashamed. In the end, Satan had no
way of making these young preachers denounce their faith
and they were released.

The great epistle on suffering in the New Testament
is 1 Peter. There is nothing heavy or oppressive about
this letter. In the very first chapter, addressing the
saints who 'have had to suffer grief in all kinds of trials',
he assures them that as they believe, they 'are filled with
an inexpressible and glorious joy'.[40] But that joy does
not necessarily follow. Let me repeat, what suffering
does for us is determined by our attitude to it, and Peter
has something vital to say to us about that.

'Therefore, since Christ suffered in his body, arm
yourselves also with the same attitude, because he who
has suffered in his body is done with sin. As a result, he
does not live the rest of his earthly life for evil human
desires, but rather for the will of God.'[41] The attitude of
our Lord is seen by the way in which he sets his face to
tread the path that led to Calvary. Suffering may destroy
a believer. Hardship may cause him to pull back. Persecution may neutralize his testimony. That is usually
Satan's purpose in mounting such attacks on the child
of God. As John writes in Revelation: 'Do not be afraid
of what you are about to suffer. I tell you, the Devil will
put some of you in prison to test you, and you will suffer

persecution for ten days. Be faithful, even to the point of death, and I will give you the crown of life.'[42]

Peter teaches us that our protective armour against such attacks is a mind-set, a heart attitude—to accept the suffering that may be required of us in fulfilling the will of God. He was well qualified to speak on this score. He could recall how he and John had been arrested for preaching in the temple courts, and brought before the Sanhedrin. They were asked in whose name they had healed the lame man. 'It is by the name of Jesus Christ of Nazareth,' answered Peter, 'whom you crucified, but whom God raised from the dead, that this man stands before you completely healed.'[43] When your Master has been executed a few weeks before by this very ruling body, you don't answer them like that unless you have armed yourself with a mind to suffer.

In the next chapter of the Acts, all the apostles are arraigned before the same body, flogged and only released after being threatened about speaking any more in the name of Jesus. We are told, 'The apostles left the Sanhedrin, rejoicing because they had been counted worthy of suffering disgrace for the Name. Day after day, in the temple courts and from house to house, they never stopped teaching and proclaiming the good news that Jesus is the Christ.'[44] You don't behave like that, however zealous, unless you are armed with a mind to suffer.

Watchman Nee ministered on this very theme before the Communist authorities shut him up in prison for twenty years. God was surely preparing him—and he was preparing the flock—for what lay ahead. He emphasized strongly that God is not against enjoyment, and will not withhold any good thing from his obedient children. But that does not prevent us from having a mind to suffer.

There is much suffering that we can avoid if we wish: but if we are to be of use to the Lord, it is a fundamental necessity that we make deliberate choice of the path of suffering for his sake. Unless we acquire a disposition to suffer for him, the work we do will be of a very superficial quality...the question is not one of the amount of suffering we may be called upon to meet, but of our attitude toward it...suffering may not be your daily portion, but you must daily be prepared to suffer.[45]

We do not know how much suffering Watchman Nee was called upon to bear, but we do know he never denied his Lord or chose the easy path of compromise to escape from prison.

Of the same spirit was the courageous Wang Mingdao. He had seen clearly that even the smallest compromise would open the way for further retreats from the truth. For him, loyalty to Jesus Christ had to have precedence over all other loyalty. Obedience to the demands of Jesus Christ inevitably brought him in conflict with the secular state. He knew full well that the course he was taking could only lead to prison, and his bag was always packed for the time when the call should come.[46]

There was nothing fatalistic about that 'packed bag'. He knew that God *could* deliver him, but God had given him no intimation that he would do so, and save him by a supernatural deliverance from what many of his compatriots were suffering. Every time he saw that packed bag it would strengthen that determination in his heart, 'I will not shrink from this path. I have a mind to suffer.' It was like this with the three Hebrews faced with the burning fiery furnace. The God, whom they served was able to deliver them. 'But even if he does not,' they said, 'we are not going to serve...the golden image.'[47] It's that little, 'But if not' clause that represents the mind to suffer.

Perhaps we feel this would all be very relevant if we were living, like the Chinese church, under a Communist regime. But how can it apply to Christians brought up in the freedom of the West? Are we to pray for persecution, court calamity or indulge in some self-inflicted suffering. No, indeed. But we are mistaken if we think that having a democratic government can guarantee us freedom from persecution. It is not only civic authorities who persecute.

I believe that God has been warning his children in the West for some years through what has been happening in Russia, in China, in Ethiopia, as well as in certain Islamic and other non-Marxist societies. Persecution for the child of God is a reality, even in the twentieth century, and we must not fool ourselves that this can never happen to us. I fear that if it did overtake us in our present state, the spiritual casualty rate would be high.

In China the issues are clear cut: to live for Jesus without compromise and confess him without fear is to suffer. For us in the West, this is not necessarily so. How then is it really possible in our situation to have a mind to suffer? In what ways are we to embrace the cross? These are questions that we must now face.

Chapter Thirteen

HOW TO EMBRACE THE CROSS

> *Therefore, since we have so great a crowd of witnesses surrounding us...let us run with endurance the race...fixing our eyes on Jesus... who for the joy set before him endured the cross.*
>
> Heb 12:1–2 (NASB)

A brilliant young Chinese scientist, converted to Christ while a student in the USA, wrote to David Adeney shortly before returning to his native Shanghai:

> I do not care whether I live six days or six years. I can only say with the apostle Paul, 'I do not count my life of any value, nor as precious to myself, if only I may accomplish my course and the ministry I have received from the Lord Jesus, to testify to the Gospel of the grace of God.'[48]

This young man, living in the easy affluence of the West, and far removed from the kind of persecution that he knew he would face back in China, had heard the call of God, and adopted a mind to suffer. To do the same is within the grasp of everyone who reads this book.

Soldiers *off* the battlefield may be able to perform their duties without any great hardship or self-denial. But *on* the battlefield hardship is a daily fact of life. For this reason, soldiers have to taste something of the rigours of the battlefield in their training. In the early days of World War Two, some allied troops in North Africa where I was serving suffered badly when they at length faced their 'baptism of fire'. They had been pampered by peacetime conditions. They were soft-bellied and vulnerable. That's the way it is with many of Christ's soldiers.

The church in China would call out to us, 'Arm yourselves with a mind to suffer.' When you hear the 'zip' of bullets or the 'crack' of exploding shells, you have left it too late. Don't wait for suffering or persecution to overtake you. Now is the time to get into training.

Soldiers of Christ are not the elite of the kingdom of God. The New Testament takes it for granted that every true believer is a soldier. To be saved is to be drafted, and you cannot separate soldiering and suffering. Paul, the seasoned warrior, reminds Timothy, his young aide, 'Take your share of suffering as a good soldier of Christ Jesus.'[49] That was something that Timothy could avoid or embrace. That's how it is with us. Is it going to take a Communist revolution to make us disciplined soldiers of Christ?

The Corinthian church was rich in spiritual gifts, but poor in self-discipline. Paul uses the figure of the Olympic games to illustrate his own experience:

Do you not know that in a race all the runners compete, but only one receives the prize? So run that you may obtain it. Every athlete exercises self-control in all things. They do it to receive a perishable wreath, but we an imperishable. Well, I do not run aimlessly, I do not box as one beating the air; but I pommel my body and subdue it, lest after preaching to others I myself should be disqualified.[50]

There are many Christians who are flabby due to over-eating and under-exercising. The physical is all too often a reflection of the spiritual. Says Paul, 'I pommel my body'—that is, 'I give it a hard time, because I want to be able to endure hardness.' God is not looking for us all to become fitness addicts. You can be an enthusiast for physical exercise and still fail to 'subdue' the body, or 'make it your slave', in the way Paul is meaning here.

It is not only on the track that the athlete trains, but also at the meal table. He avoids over-eating and late rising. Many Christians visibly wilt if called upon to sacrifice their creature comforts and endure a little hardship in the work of God. Others who are not generally self-indulgent, do have their weak spots, where they regularly give in to some fad of the body. If you're aiming for gold in the Olympics, you can't afford that weak spot. It must be 'self-control in *all things*', says Paul. With most of us there are practical issues in which we need to take ourselves in hand. Jesus taught us that if we really want to shoulder the cross, we *must* learn to say no to self.[51]

Many of us do not seem to realize that we have a war on our hands. In the face of those insatiable appetites that 'wage war against the soul',[52] our policy is to give in rather than dig in. It's time we ceased to treat our self-indulgences as a bit of a joke, and began to take this teaching of Paul seriously. It is time for pommelling that body of ours and putting it through its paces. It is an aspect of growing up.

The apostle is not here advocating the path of asceticism, which implies that the body is inherently sinful and must be constantly punished. It is not a call to exchange a nightshirt for a hairshirt! It is true that God 'richly provides us with everything for our enjoyment', but enjoyment is not to become indulgence. That happens when the body unseats the spirit and takes over the saddle. The vital question is, 'Who is in control?'

For the athlete in training the issue is very simple. He knows that if the body has not learned to take orders *off the track*, it will not respond to orders *on the track*, and that supreme effort will not be forthcoming when it is needed. Watchman Nee was a Chinese leader who had earned the right to speak on this matter. In an address to his fellow workers he said this:

> Brothers and sisters, if you have not yet brought your body under control, you had better call a halt in the work and gain dominion over it before you try to exercise authority in any wider realm. You may take great pleasure in the work, but it will have little value if you are dominated by your physical cravings. Serving the Lord is not a mere matter of preaching sermons from the platform. Paul knew that.[53]

There is a New Testament ruggedness that many of these Chinese Christians have developed that makes our western Christianity look a little anaemic. Take this report from Inner Mongolia, where three pastors in their seventies were released from labour camps. All of them had served in excess of twenty years. But they were just thrilled to serve God among the house churches. Said one of them:

> We are old, but not too old to baptize. Our last baptismal service was held in a freezing pond. The Lord enabled us to stay in the water for almost an hour!

I wonder how many converts the three of them baptized in an hour!

This pommelling of the body may be a little painful, but it is having the mind to suffer, as Jesus did. In this our Lord showed the perfect balance. We may be sure that he enjoyed his meal when he sat to eat with the tax gatherers and the sinners. He certainly wasn't an ascetic. He wasn't even a teetotaller. This gave the Pharisees the opportunity to accuse him of excess, calling him 'a glutton and a drunkard'. The truth was, he never failed to exercise the most exemplary control over his body.

Hungry and weary at Sychar's Well, Jesus refused the disciples' invitation to take food. There was a spiritual harvest, dead ripe for the reaping, so even the cry of the body for food must be made to wait. 'I have food to eat,' he explained to his disciples, 'that you know nothing about.'[54]

In the Garden of Gethsemane Jesus called to his disciples to watch and pray with him. That meant saying no to the craving for sleep. As so often happens with us, they went to sleep. 'The Spirit is willing but the body is weak,' said Jesus.[55] Here Watchman Nee asks the pertinent question, 'What is the good of a willing spirit, if the body is weak? If you are to watch with the Lord when he requires it, you will need a willing body as well as a willing spirit.'[56] That means a body that has been disciplined, that has been buffeted into submission and readily responds to the dictates of your spirit.

This emphasis on the believer's need to embrace the cross, so strongly emphasized in the New Testament epistles, seems hardly to find a place in Christian teaching today. Is it that we have graduated out of all that, and are now into the much more exciting and attractive teaching about prosperity? If we have faith, we are told, we can escape from 'the poverty trap' and enjoy material abundance. This teaching is not altogether wrong, but it is a lop-sided emphasis. It

seriously lacks the balance of the cross of which the New
Testament is so full. If we believe that the wealth of the
nations is to flow to the church, that is not intended to
produce a generation of wealthy Christians.

The New Testament does not teach that poverty is 'a
crippling curse', and that to escape from it must be a
spiritual priority. How was it that the One who became
poor for us, who had 'nowhere to lay his head', who had
to ask for a penny from the congregation to illustrate his
point, did not seem to have this prosperity faith? And
how could Paul speak of being so content 'whether well
fed or hungry, whether living in plenty or in want'?[57]
Poverty is only a trap when we face it with unbelief. The
apostle faced his times of want with the same glad
submission and buoyant faith as his times of abundance.
He had to prove God in both experiences.

Paul was certainly not speaking disparagingly of his
apostolic ministry, but rather commending it when he
said, 'To this very hour we go hungry and thirsty, we
are in rags, we are brutally treated, we are homeless.'[58]
I wonder if there are any budding apostles around who
eagerly aspire to this sort of apostolic qualification!

When Paul prayed for deliverance from his 'thorn in
the flesh'—whatever that was—God said to him, 'My
grace is sufficient for you, for my power is made perfect
in weakness.'[59] Here it comes again, the embracing of
the cross that brings a release of the power of God.
'Therefore,' says Paul, 'I will boast all the more gladly
about my weaknesses, so that Christ's power may rest
on me. That is why, for Christ's sake, I *delight* in weaknesses, in insults, in hardships, in persecutions, in difficulties.'[60]

'Just a moment, Paul, what you really mean is that
you are willing to put up with them while you call on the
Lord for speedy deliverance.'

'No, I don't. I mean what I said. I *delight* in weaknesses, in insults, in hardships, in persecutions, in difficulties. For when I am weak, then I am strong.'

As I was writing this chapter I read in a Christian magazine: 'Testings, trials and pressures do not come from God, and are not designed by God to perfect you.' The writer exhorted us to get out of our thinking immediately that they are part of the 'all things that work together for good'. I found myself asking, does this exponent of the faith message have a different Bible from mine? He was insisting that the only proper mental attitude to such things was: 'This is not of God; it is Satan and I fully expect God to deliver me.' Faith for instant deliverance was the only course. Faith to endure was not an option.

This is not the balanced emphasis on faith given us in either the Old or New Testament. Take the heroes of faith listed in Hebrews 11. Not all get a mention in the record because of *the faith of their achievement*; some are listed because of *the faith of their endurance*. By faith some 'escaped the edge of the sword', while others, equally men of faith, were 'put to death by the sword'. There were those who 'went about in sheepskins and goatskins, destitute, persecuted and ill-treated'.[61] Hardly a good advertisement for material prosperity, or for deliverance from 'testings, trials and pressures' yet the inspired writer reserves for them this final accolade—'the world was not worthy of them'.

It is our love of a smooth, trouble-free ride that causes us to shrink from the cross of Christ. If we are going to shoulder a cross at all, we want it planed and polished, not the old rugged cross that Jesus bore. Those sort chafe the shoulder and leave splinters in the fingers. No, it is not poverty that hinders us embracing the cross, but our affluence, and the materialistic spirit that so often goes with it.

Very few Chinese believers are materially prosperous. Many are very poor, even by Chinese standards. But I believe the head of the church says to them, as he said to the suffering church of Smyrna: 'I know your afflictions and your poverty—yet you are rich!'[62] This is surely true New Testament prosperity. 'Has not God chosen those who are poor in the eyes of the world to be'—not materially wealthy, but—'rich in faith and to inherit the kingdom.'[63]

If we were presented with a choice, would we prefer to be like the Smyrnans, rich in faith but materially poor, or like the Laodicians, poor in faith but materially rich? 'When it comes to spiritual or material wealth,' someone would be quick to tell us, 'it doesn't have to be either/or, it should be both'. For some that may be true, but did the Father give his Son that option? Did the Christians who were told in the Hebrew epistle, 'you joyfully accepted the confiscation of your property', have that option? Their joy was not, 'because you have faith for those goods to be speedily replaced, and even more to be given you', but—'because you knew that you yourselves had better and lasting possessions'.[64]

'Prosperity,' we are told, 'is not to make us rich for ourselves, but that we might be rich towards God and give generously to his work.' Fine, but how many Christians respond to this because their single motive is to give more, and how many because it also holds out the prospect of improving their own living standards? The gift of giving in the New Testament, mentioned alongside such gifts as prophesying, serving and teaching,[65] is a faith ministry that does not need to operate out of abundance.

The greatest givers in Scripture, according to heaven's estimate, were poor. Take the little widow who put her 'two mites' into the treasury. It was 'all she had to live on', and no one would ever have known, if Jesus had not revealed it. But it was he who said that she had given more than all the rich.[66] Or the Macedonian Christians of whom Paul said, 'Out of the most severe trial, their overflowing joy and their extreme poverty welled up in rich generosity. For I testify that they gave as much as they were able, and even beyond their ability. Entirely on their own, they urgently pleaded with us for the privilege of sharing in this service to the saints.'[67] That's the kind of giving that makes heaven sit up and take notice, and you'll find more of it in China than in the affluent West.

If God gives us material wealth as we seek first his kingdom, then that is good. There will be grace to use it aright, to advance the kingdom and not wither our spiritual life. In itself it is not a goal of faith to be sought. It can be a dangerous teaching if no mention is made of the many biblical warnings about the love of riches. And those who append to their teaching an appeal for funds—'Give to this work of mine, and see how God will prosper you!'—must not be surprised if their motives are questioned.

To live simply and modestly in an affluent society is costly. It takes the cross of Christ to put to death that acquisitive spirit, and to bring us into that place of contentment. Paul warned Timothy of those 'who think that godliness is a means to financial gain' and went on to say, that 'if we have food and clothing'—please note the 'if'—'we will be content with that.'[68]

There is another vital area where we may, if we will, embrace the cross. Bodily suffering may not be our lot just now, but mental suffering is always with us, and some Christians cannot cope with it. Solomon reminds us, if we should need reminding, 'rash words are like sword thrusts'.[69] Thoughtless behaviour may deeply wound. Unchristianlike attitudes may cause grievous suffering. All that has been said about bodily suffering equally applies to mental suffering. What it does to you and in you—what, if anything, it accomplishes for the kingdom of God—depends upon the way you respond to it.

We cannot avoid being hurt. It is an occupational hazard of living in an imperfect world. But there is nothing accidental about it. It *is*, despite what the magazine article may say, part of God's providential ordering of our lives, and therefore contains potential blessing. 'Those who suffer according to God's will'— that is suffering that is not the result of our own sin or stupidity—'should commit themselves to their faithful Creator and continue to do good.'[70]

Where there is a failure to arm yourself with a mind to suffer, words, actions and attitudes that cause suffering become a battleground for defeat instead of for victory. Your unseemly reactions become as unspiritual as the words and actions that cause them; and Satan wins a two-fold victory. The wound quickly becomes infected with hurt pride, anger and resentment. If you still do not take action, bitterness, self-pity and unforgiveness will set in.

From then on everything that that one who hurt you says or does is viewed with a jaundiced eye. You don't want to hear anything good about him. Any success he has will only be 'temporary'. Any kindness he performs will have 'a dubious motive'. Nothing that he does will be right. Your judgement will be warped by your own prejudices.

These hurts are in most cases a mere pinprick compared with what many Chinese believers have suffered. Are you thinking that it must be easier to take persecutions from the world than to take hurts from your fellow Christians, or those who are particularly close? But these are the very hurts that many of the saints in China have experienced. Unfortunately not all believers there have been faithful to God, and to their brothers and sisters in Christ. There have been many betrayals, and many accusations of believers by believers.

Many a pastor or preacher has been dragged before a public meeting convened to accuse him, to find that some of his own flock, even those whom he had led to Christ, were there to speak against him in front of the unbelieving Communists. Watchman Nee and Wang Mingdao experienced it. And it wasn't only leaders who suffered in this way. Many ordinary believers were betrayed by fellow Christians. It was not just the humiliation and public dishonouring that they had to suffer. There often followed years in jail or hard labour camp, separated from family and loved ones. Plenty of time to let the gall of it get into your soul, if you allowed that to happen. That so many came through it with a beautiful Christlike spirit was only because they had armed themselves with 'a mind to suffer'.

There is nothing more destructive of relationships in the body of Christ than the way that Christians react to hurts, usually thoughtless rather than malicious. God is calling us to get into training, to have a mind to suffer for his sake—to embrace the cross. But how do we do it? Peter and Paul were well qualified to answer.

1. Make sure that your suffering is not something you have foolishly brought on yourself. There is no value in that kind of suffering.[71]

2. If you suffer because you are a Christian, you are to praise God that you bear his name. You are suffering in his will, and you can commit your cause to him.[72]

3. Do not let suffering, of whatever sort, take you by

surprise, or think it strange. Rejoice in the privilege of sharing in Christ's sufferings. You are not being singled out for special punishment, but for special blessing. The Spirit of glory is resting on you.[73]

4. Take your eyes off the cause of the suffering, and become 'conscious of God' in that situation. You are following in the footsteps of Christ.[74]

5. When you suffer for right, you may be hurt, but you cannot be harmed. You are, in fact, blessed. Seize the opportunity this may bring to witness.[75]

6. Don't retaliate or seek vengeance, but commit the issues to God who judges justly, even as Jesus did.[76]

7. Don't develop a martyr spirit or join in 'the pity party'. View your suffering as a small thing. What is it in comparison with Christ's suffering? How does it even compare with Paul's and his fellow workers', which he described as 'our light and momentary troubles'! Get taken up with the 'eternal glory that far outweighs them all'.[77]

8. Aim at coming to that place where you can say with Paul, 'I *delight*' in all these sufferings because in this kind of weakness I am really strong.[78]

Was Paul not referring to the marks of suffering when he closed his epistle to the Galatians with these words— 'I bear on my body the marks of Jesus'? Do you bear any mark of suffering?

> Hast thou no wound?
> Yet I was wounded by the archers, spent,
> Lean me against a tree to die; and rent
> By ravening beasts that compassed me, I swooned;
> Hast thou no wound?
>
> Hast thou no scar?
> No hidden scar on foot or side or hand?

I hear thee sung as mighty in the land,
I hear them hail thy bright ascendant star,
Hast thou no scar?

No wound? No scar?
Yet, as the Master shall the servant be,
And pierced are the feet that follow me;
But thine are whole: can he have followed far
Who has nor wound nor scar?

Amy Carmichael

Chapter Fourteen

DYNAMIC PRAYING

After they prayed, the place where they were
meeting was shaken. And they were all filled with
the Holy Spirit and spoke the word of God boldly.

Acts 4:31

That early record gives us some challenging insights
into the prayer life of those first Christians. Not only
was the early church born out of the womb of prayer,
but by prayer was fed and nurtured. It was on their
knees that they met those first blasts of the Enemy's
counter attack, whether persecution from without or
dissension from within. The church in China was also
born out of prayer, and sacrificial praying has characterized it from the start.

Pastor Hsi was a contemporary of the early missionary pioneers, like Hudson Taylor. He was a Con-
fucian scholar and an opium addict when God saved
him. From the time of his conversion and early deliverance from opium addiction, he adopted the name
Sheng-mo, meaning 'conqueror of demons', in the
conviction that what God had done for him he would,
by God's grace, do for others.

Within a few months of his own deliverance his wife,
as yet unconverted, became uncontrollably demonized.

Hsi called for a fast for three days and nights in his household. He then laid hands on his wife, and in the name of Jesus commanded the evil spirits to depart and torment her no more. Mrs Hsi was delivered instantly and permanently, and became his devoted partner in the work.

From then on, conflict with the powers of darkness was very much the characteristic of this man's ministry. Great was the power of Satan let loose against him, but greater was the power of God to save, deliver and heal. Churches were established throughout the whole region as a result of his ministry. Whatever the crisis—the need of divine guidance or wisdom, the deliverance of opium addicts, or those otherwise demonized, the withstanding of opposition—Hsi had only one solution. He gave himself to prayer and fasting. What mighty victories and deliverances God wrought for him and through him!

God caused the church in China to flex her prayer muscles and to prove him with remarkable answers to prayer in the pre-revolutionary period. Watchman Nee tells a story of how, in the early days of the work, he and six other brothers went on a preaching tour to an island off the South China coast.

There was little response to their preaching. Wu was the youngest in the team, only sixteen and newly converted. He asked the crowd why they would not believe. They replied that they already had a god, Ta-wang (meaning Great King). For centuries they celebrated his festival every January on a day revealed by divination. It was always a perfectly fine day. On learning that the festival was fixed for January 11th, in two days' time, Wu boldly declared: 'I promise you it will rain on the 11th.'

'That is enough!' retorted the crowd. 'We don't want

to hear any more preaching. If there is rain on the 11th, then your God is God!'

The news spread like wildfire. Wu's rash prediction had put the older Christians, Watchman Nee included, on the spot. They stopped their preaching and gave themselves to prayer. God gave Watchman Nee the words, 'Where is the God of Elijah?' He now felt assured that God would send rain on the 11th. They thanked God and went out to broadcast their acceptance of the devil's challenge.

That evening, as doubts began to assail, they went back to prayer, 'We want rain—*now*, Lord.' Again the word came, 'Where is the God of Elijah?' They felt rebuked. They confessed their sin of unbelief and acknowledged that they did not need rain until the time of the procession, eight o'clock in the morning on the 11th.

On the morning of the 11th Watchman Nee was awakened by the rays of the sun. It was already past seven o'clock. 'This isn't rain, Lord, please send the rain!'

Back came the word, 'Where is the God of Elijah?'

Humbled, he walked silently down to breakfast. Everyone was very quiet as they took their place at the table. There was not a cloud in the sky. As they bowed to say grace, they reminded God of his promise, and before they could say 'Amen' they heard the first drops of rain on the tiles. There was a steady shower as they took their first bowl of rice.

In the village, some of the younger generation looked at that first shower and said, 'There is God. No more Ta-wang! He is kept in by the rain.' But the faithful brought him out on a sedan chair. Surely he will stop the rain. Back at the breakfast table the team said grace again for their second bowl of rice! This time they asked God for heavier rain. Before their breakfast was finished it was coming down in bucketfuls, and the street was deep in water.

The procession had only proceeded a few yards when the coolies stumbled and fell. Poor Ta-wang had his jaw and left arm fractured. Emergency repairs were quickly carried out. Slipping and stumbling the coolies carried him half-way round the village, then the floods defeated them. Some of the village elders, bare-headed and without umbrellas because of their faith in Ta-wang's weather, had also fallen and were in serious difficulty— in more ways than one!

The idol was taken into a home where they 'divined' thay they had got the day wrong. January 14th at six o'clock in the evening was the proper time for the procession. 'Lord, send rain on the 14th, but give us four good days till then,' the workers prayed. That very afternoon the skies cleared and the weather was fine for the next few days. The 14th broke, bright and clear. Again at the appointed time, they reminded God of his promises. Not a minute late the answer came with torrential rain and floods. The power of Ta-wang was broken.[79]

Undoubtedly the pressure of the persecution has deepened and intensified the prayer life of the Chinese church. It was a slow process which began after the terrible 1966-69 period of the Cultural Revolution. A few servants of God, moved by the spiritual desolation they faced, began to pray for revival. They urged others to cast off their fears and do the same. These small secret prayer groups grew into Spirit-filled house churches. Deprived of 'ordained' leaders, 'lay' leaders rose up to take their place. The Spirit of God was moving all over China, and house churches sprang up in every city, town and countless villages. The new Chinese church was born out of the womb of prayer.

In a coastal city in 1967, the resumption of small

meetings had brought a time of intense opposition and persecution. Over a period of three months the churches were called by their pastors to engage in prayer and fasting. Believers were being humiliated, tortured and threatened. Many died in prison, while others were killed or crippled by savage beatings. Then in 1978 a powerful work of the Holy Spirit brought thousands to Christ. One city reports 50,000 Christians meeting in 600 households, that constitutes one in eight, or 12.5% of the population. Even children remained true to the Lord, despite being threatened by their teachers.

According to the United Nations' latest estimate, one out of three persons in China are under fifteen. That means that there are about 300 million children in China. No wonder the authorities insist that no one under eighteen is allowed to attend church or be taught the gospel. Christian children at a very young age have to learn how to protect their parents and families. 'Whenever a stranger stepped into our home,' said a five-year-old to a staff member of Christian Communications, 'I would see if he was for us or against us.'

'How could you tell?' she asked the child.

'I'll pray and the Lord will tell me,' was the answer.

'How do you pray?' was the next question.

Smiling, the little girl replied, 'Oh, you won't know when I am praying because I pray in my heart.'

There was a Christian lady who returned from overseas to her native village in 1974, fearful of what she might find. She found eighty rejoicing believers with a strong pure faith. Those who had been sent to prison had witnessed to other prisoners. Prayer and fasting were normal activities in the village, and God was demonstrating his power to heal, and confounding the scepticism of the unbelievers.

In some communities Christians meet every day to

pray for their country. Those who have been privileged to meet with them speak of the spirit of urgency that characterizes their praying. Most unlikely converts become praying saints. Take the case of the old man who had been troubled by a demon. After the demon was cast out he turned to the Lord and became a dedicated believer. He deeply desired to serve the Lord, but was told there was little he could do. Then he began to rise at four o'clock every morning to pray. Now he recognizes that this is the ministry to which God has called him.

One who has researched the growth of the house churches describes the 'disciplined prayer life' of believers as its distinguishing feature. There is nothing inward looking or self-centred about the way they pray. Their prayer life reaches around the world. In one of China's most important cities a group meets every Saturday from nine in the morning till three or later in the afternoon for a time of prayer and fasting. On this occasion their primary request was that Bible Schools and Seminaries in the West would remain true to the word of God.

Here are some sample prayer requests from a house church:

May the Lord enable me to have spiritual wisdom to expound the gospel clearly and fully. Oh for the gift of raising high the cross! Oh for the power of the Holy Spirit when preaching the cross, that all men may be drawn to the Lord by the power of the cross.

May the Lord give preaching ability to expose sin, to make men fear. And the help of the Spirit that men may be convicted of sin, and righteousness and of judgement, and so earnestly repent.

May the Lord continually place a spirit of awe in my heart, so that I may obtain humility, and also grow daily in wisdom and knowledge.

May the Lord grant me by his grace, the ability to obey his Holy Spirit, so that I can strengthen my brethren.

For the gift of establishing and pastoring of the church and for prophetic preaching.

For the fullness of the Spirit.

For a willingness to suffer.

May the Lord control my tongue to speak words that will build up others.

May the Lord enable me not to love the world or its empty glory, but to be bold and be completely committed to God.

May I have the gift of praising God and of spiritual songs.

We have earlier spoken of the revival in Henan (Honan) Province. It seems that God is continuing to affirm his word with signs and wonders. Although the majority of believers are farmers and ordinary peasants, many Communist Party members, cadres, brigade leaders and other officials are turning to Christ. With many it is the result of miracles.

People of Henan are very simple, honest and frank. This is a quality that makes it easier for them to receive the gospel, and when they pray they take everything, great or small, to the Lord, believing for an answer. In one village there was a plague of rats that brought much destruction and sickness. The Christians prayed and within days all the rats mysteriously died.

Many people who have had terminal illnesses have been healed through the prayers of the Christians. One brother known to a Hong Kong pastor with whom I spoke, was paralyzed and bed-ridden for many years before his salvation. After receiving Christ he was totally healed, and recently travelled the long journey to Guanzhou (Canton) to pick up Bibles. It was here he met brothers from Hong Kong to whom he told his story.

David Wang, brought up in Shanghai, recalls the neighbour who had a little house built in her garden when she became a Christian. This was used by visiting pastors as 'a prophets' chamber', but it was also used as a place for fasting and prayer. 'I remember Christians,' recalls David, 'including my mother, who would go to "the little ark" as it was called, and for days they would pray and fast. Even as a young boy I would sense the fervency of their prayers—a fervency that has never left China's Christians.'

On a recent visit to China with a co-worker, David visited a lady who had just been released after twenty-three years in prison. They brought her food, medicine, clothing, money and of course a Bible. 'That woman was a saint!' recalled David. Before they left she requested prayer with the visitors. Very softly she began to pray. They felt as though 'the ions and molecules of the atmosphere were suddenly charged'. It seemed as though they could 'sense the vibrations of the presence of God'.

David was reminded of those first Christians: 'After they prayed, the place where they were meeting was shaken.' They could sense the moving and the shaking in the spiritual realm, as though this little woman was attacking the very gates of hell. 'Though she prayed so softly, she was perspiring all over. We were immersed in an atmosphere of grace, communion and intercession in spiritual warfare. She was reminding God of his promises and pledging her obedience to his word.' They left the room of her little shack awed, as though they had been in the vestibule of heaven.

Without doubt here in the West we are seeing God moving by his Holy Spirit. Many of us have become accustomed to attend celebrations and conventions that would be described as 'charismatic'. Generally the atmosphere has been good, the worship lively and the gifts of the Spirit in evidence. The preaching of the word has been blessed, even anointed. Conversions, healings and deliverances have been witnessed. But the whole operation has been largely man-centred, need-centred and result-centred. We have looked to the charisma of the speaker to 'draw in the net' and produce results, with the help of counsellors. The measure of visible blessing may vary, but the manner of the Spirit's operation has become predictable. We almost know before-hand what will happen and we now have a generation of believers who don't expect anything more.

Is not the vital missing element that awesome, sub-duing, melting, overwhelming Presence, that undefin-able element that transforms a meeting from being man-centred to being God-centred? It lifts it from the mundane to the sublime and from the expected to the spontaneous and the unpredictable. It may release God's people into rhapsodies of praise, where they feel as though they have joined the angelic choirs. Or it may prostrate them on their faces in an awed silence at the presence of his Majesty. Anxiety about results will then be far from their thinking. All will be taken up with God. It will be enough to know that he who is 'majestic in holiness, awesome in glory, working wonders'[80] has taken the field.

Who will deny that this is the God of the Bible? This is how he has come again and again in Scripture and in history. Why do we so rarely experience it? Is it not because we know so little about the kind of praying described in this chapter. The leaders just haven't time. They are much too busy with their schedules and their programmes. And the people, who take their cue from the leaders, are likewise caught up in a busy round of activities. No one has time for this kind of praying.

If we are ever to know the presence of the God of majesty and might we must adjust our thinking, and discover where our priorities really lie. The Holy Spirit wants to lead us into this dynamic praying, but before that can happen we must let him destroy our self-satisfaction with what we are currently seeing. The basis of such a rediscovery of God is holy discontent and heart hunger. 'You will seek me and find me when you seek me *with all your heart*.'[81]

Chapter Fifteen

INTENSE HUNGER

*Your statutes are wonderful; therefore I obey them.
The unfolding of your words gives light; it gives
understanding to the simple. I open my mouth and
pant, longing for your commands.*

Psalm 119:129–131

A young refugee from China, who had found Christ in
the People's Republic two years before, was asked by
Paul Kauffman whether he owned a Bible.

'No,' he replied.

'A New Testament?'

'No.'

'Did you have any Christian literature as a new
convert?'

'Yes. An old lady who was a Christian tore one page
out of her daily devotional book and gave it to me.'[82]

Here is the first reason for the intense hunger of
Chinese believers for the word of God—the acute lack of
Bibles and Christian literature. It is a strange fact of life
that we do not value many of the precious things we
have until we find ourselves deprived of them. Here in
the West we are surfeited with Bibles, most of us have
two or three, with Christian literature of every conceivable kind. How much do we really value it all?

Here is a recent letter from a north-western province signed by one who calls himself Brother Zhu:

> The Spirit of the Lord has fallen upon us in these last days. Many of our young people have been filled with the Holy Spirit and are willing to dedicate their lives to God. We cannot but give thanks to God. This last time when we met in a certain county 125 people received water baptism, and about 600 came to our gatherings. Today our congregation registers about 1,000. The Holy Spirit works mightily. It is difficult for me to describe the urgency of the needs here. When the people see and hear the word of God, there are tears of joy flowing down many of their faces. Their joy is beyond what words could express.

The other factor behind this hunger is the powerful moving of the Holy Spirit. Hunger for God is a hallmark of revival, and wherever there is hunger for God there is hunger for his word. It is the work of the Holy Spirit to break down our complacency and lethargy and to give us a spiritual hunger for the things of God. 'Oh no, not another meeting!' is a comment often thought, if not expressed, among western Christians. Among the Chinese house churches you will hear the eager question, 'When is the next meeting?'

> In many places Bibles are too scarce and too precious even to be taken to the Christian gatherings. A government raid on the meeting place is always a danger, so all that is brought to the meeting is notebooks into which the Scriptures are handcopied.

Before the Revolution God had raised up in China a number of great teachers and evangelists, like John Sung, Wang Mingdao and Watchman Nee. Their ministry, however, was similar to men in the West with a fine pulpit ministry which held captive large congregations, who came week by week to be fed. But the situation in China has changed all that. The great men have all been arrested. The great names have gone. The church in the house has compelled the whole body of Christ to function. In place of the big preacher God is raising up a multitude of new ministries, teachers and preachers. A house church will often devote one night a week to learning the art of preaching or how to share the gospel with others.

All this does not mean that they do not value highly the visits of those who have an anointed ministry in the word of God. Rather the reverse, as the following reveals:

> A preacher was invited for the day to a small town to hold meetings. At dawn, the building was crammed with 600 people, with others packed into the courtyard outside. They were willing to suffer the extremely cold weather in order to hear the Lord's message. Before the preacher arrived they sang hymns in order to prepare their hearts to receive the word of God. The preacher spoke three times and the Christians sat and listened from early morning until late at night. Still they did not want to disperse. They plucked his sleeve, saying, 'We have never heard such good preaching.' They were extraordinarily eager to hear Bible truth expounded.

One itinerant preacher recounted how, when asked what was his subject he replied, 'About Jesus Christ in the book of Matthew.'

'Oh,' they replied, 'he is going to preach the book of Matthew. The entire book is about Jesus Christ!' They held him to his word. Thirty-seven hours later he finished a verse by verse exposition of the life of Jesus Christ in the book of Matthew.[83]

A sister in Christ who was able to spend a good deal

of time in China between 1980 and 1982, a period when there was rapid expansion among the house churches, tells how she attended an ordination service in a house church. There were twelve pastors and house church leaders present. They were ordaining a farmer from the countryside who had been converted in 1962 by reading a Bible loaned to him by an elderly Christian woman. She eventually gave him the Bible fearing that the Red Guards might find it and burn it, as this was the time of the Cultural Revolution.

As the believers grew in number, the farmer saw that teaching was as important as evangelizing. With only a few Bibles in the whole village, how were the people to be taught? He was led to compile a topical Bible handbook, which took him seven years to complete. It took so long because every time his then unconverted wife found the book she would tear it up or burn it. In addition to that difficulty, the only time for writing was between the end of his daily work and sunset, as they had no electricity in the country. On completion the book was mimeographed by the believers, and 10,000 copies had been distributed in ten prefectures within that province. The pastors and leaders felt that this man had qualified for ordination!

The same sister heard an itinerant preacher from Shanghai tell of his visit to a village in Henan (Honan) Province. He was a stranger there, and the villagers took him to their home, and into a room with Scriptures plastered all over the walls. They wanted to share the gospel with him. When they found out that he was a Christian they immediately asked him to preach. They took him to a room where another preacher was concluding his message to 400 or more people. The congregation was overflowing into the yard. He took over and preached from nine in the morning till eleven at night. Then the believers asked him to spend the night with an elderly woman, and preach again next day.

He was awakened in the middle of the night and given a full breakfast at four in the morning. Then they rushed him to another meeting which was to start at six o'clock. To satisfy their great hunger for God's word without disrupting production the believers will often gather together hours before they work, and then again hours after they finish.

The preacher reported that in this particular village Christians will hang posters on their doors to proclaim their faith in Christ. He saw only three doors without posters. These, he was told, were the homes of former landlords who were still hesitant to be bold in their testimony because of their 'bad record'. He was told that even the Public Security Chief was a secret believer, and would not persecute the Christians.

When you get this kind of hunger for the word of God, you need have no fear as to how people respond when that word is brought to them. Wang Mindao was only released from prison in 1980 at eighty years of age. He had spent twenty-four years in prison. David Wang visited him in his little room in Shanghai. He was already half-blind and in feeble health, suffering from a number of illnesses. David asked this Mr Valiant-for-Truth why it was the church in China was experiencing 'such magnificent and glorious interventions by God'. 'Well,' he said, 'we have no Bible, no church, no missionaries, no Bible schools, no seminaries. Perhaps it is because we have nothing that God has special mercy on us. He has given us the faith of a mustard seed, simple child-like trust in him. The Chinese Christians just believe God and his word. We believe that he is able and willing to do great things for us.'

Speaking further on this very matter of response to the word, David recounts a visit he made to a remote region of North West China, where he preached for about three hours to seventy young people. His theme was 'the Lord's prayer'. They were sitting all over the floor or leaning against the wall of the little mud hut. They were not just listening, they were writing down every word—and they were weeping.

When he had finished, the house church leader gave him some tea, saying 'After you've had tea you can preach to us again.' That was after three hours of solid preaching! He took his tea and then preached for another four or five hours. All the time the young people were taking down notes, and echoing, 'Amen! Amen!' Finally he sat down totally exhausted.

'Now let us sing,' said the leader.

David was shocked as he heard the words of their song:

> Don't listen to sermons; don't listen to sermons;
> We will not listen to sermons....

What kind of response was this to his two sermons lasting seven or eight hours? Then came their real response as they sung with heart and soul, clenching their fists:

> We will live out the sermons! We will live out the sermons!

He went away knowing that they would do just that.

The fervent praying and the insatiable appetite for the word of God that we have recounted in these two chapters simply tell us that these Chinese believers are *hungry for God*—hungry in a way that we seldom see in the church at large. Their readiness to embrace the cross and to suffer, their determination to witness, their eagerness and fervency in prayer, their love of the fellowship of the saints, their longing for more and more of

God's word, and their whole-hearted response to that word—all speak of a heart attitude to God.

Here in the West, we have the same Bible, the same access to God in prayer, the same—or more—opportunity for fellowship, the same Holy Spirit. Why then do we not see this same hunger? Is it not that we have so much to take away our spiritual appetite? Whether we are moving in what are called evangelical, renewal, Pentecostal or restoration circles, the situation is largely the same. The church has been invaded by a subtle influence that is 'not of the Father, but is of the world', and most of us are unaware that we have been affected by it.

In many quarters there has been a strong reaction to certain evangelical anti-worldly teaching of the past. For example, if you were a 'keen Christian' there were 'worldly things' you didn't do. It was right to reject that approach as being negative and legalistic. Paul rejected it when he wrote:

> Since you died with Christ to the basic principles of this world, why, as though you still belonged to it, do you submit to its rules: 'Do not handle! Do not taste! Do not touch!'? These are all destined to perish with use, because they are based on human commands and teachings.[84]

We saw that one could avoid these things and still be worldly. They were not the criteria of true spirituality. Who could prove from Scripture which of these 'evangelical taboos', if any, were wrong? Did we not have liberty to follow our conscience in these areas, without being looked down upon by other Christians?

These were all valid questions, but in a subtle way our view of the world began to change. Of course it had its unacceptable face, but it wasn't really too bad a spot to be in, especially if you were in the 'prosperity league' and could afford to live well. With all the exciting new truth about the triumph of the kingdom of God, Scriptures that spoke about out attitude to this world were seldom mentioned:

My kingdom is not of this world.[85]

Seek first his kingdom and his righteousness, and all these things [the necessities of life] will be given to you as well.[86]

See the things that are above, where Christ is.... Set your minds on things that are above.[87]

Do not love the world, or anything in the world. If anyone loves the world, the love of the Father is not in him.[88]

The world and its desires pass away, but the man who does the will of God lives forever.[89]

The thought that as Christians we were 'aliens and strangers in the world',[90] and that 'our citizenship is in heaven'[91] did not hold any great appeal. We had so much going for us down here. Other-worldliness appeared to us as a form of super-spirituality. We did not want anyone thinking that we were 'heavenly minded, and no earthly use'. We failed to see that our reaction placed us in a far greater danger of being so earthly-minded we were no heavenly use!

On top of this there was little or nothing said about the place of the cross in Christian experience, a point we have already made. The cross not only shapes our thinking about sin, about suffering, about the law, but about the world as well. It settles for ever what must be our attitude to the world. What Paul said about our not submitting to rules, regulations and Thou-shalt-nots was based on the understanding that we had died to the basic principles of the world. But if we have not embraced the cross, our new found 'liberty' will never prevent the world and its spirit penetrating our spiritual defences. Paul himself had got right through on this issue, for he wrote:

> May I never boast except in the cross of our Lord Jesus Christ, through which the world has been crucified to me, and I to the world.[92]

Christians today—whether evangelical, charismatic or 'restoration'—need to be crucified to the world, and the world crucified to them. They are tasting the world—always of course in moderation—and they have lost their hunger for God. The Chinese church by contrast, teaches the cross, embraces the cross, dies to the world, lives in heaven—with feet firmly on earth, and has this insatiable hunger for God.

Chapter Sixteen

WHERE SUPERNATURAL IS NATURAL

Now, Lord, consider their threats and enable your servants to speak your word with great boldness. Stretch out your hand to heal and perform miraculous signs and wonders through the name of your holy servant Jesus.

Acts 4:29–30

Long before the Communist Revolution, healings and deliverance from demonism had often accompanied work in China. This we have already noticed in connection with the ministry of Pastor Hsi. But during the long dark night of the Cultural Revolution, and the years of rapid church expansion that have followed, supernatural manifestations, especially healings, have become a prominent feature of the movement of the Spirit.

The Acts of the Apostles records many significant thrusts of the Holy Spirit that resulted in a harvest of conversions and accelerated the progress of the kingdom. It is significant that every one of these was precipitated by some supernatural display of God's power. As we have been reminded by the words at the head of this chapter, this was what those early Christians asked God to do, and this was exactly what he did in response.

Here is another remarkable similarity between the early church and the church in China today.

Speaking of the regular occurrence of healing and miracles in his fellowship, a Christian leader in China said, 'Our believers just simply trust the Lord like little children trusting their father. And our heavenly Father cares and loves us so much he often heals our sick and meets our needs.' Or as a Chinese worker, who is constantly in and out of China, put it to me in Hong Kong: 'The Christians on the mainland do not consider these things unusual. To them the supernatural has become natural.'

Although simplicity of faith is a great quality, unless it is rooted in sound biblical teaching, it can lead to superstition and credulity. Where God is at work, Satan necessarily has his counterfeits. There are many so-called 'faith healers', witches and fortune-tellers in China, and because of lack of teaching among many professing Christians, they can be gullible and vulnerable. The Communists are very ready to seize upon these counterfeits and use them to discredit the real manifestations of the Holy Spirit.

It is obvious that a Communistic government will view all healings and miracles as mere superstition. A Christian I heard about who travels regularly behind the Iron Curtain, has now been banned from East Germany because of a recent visit when miracles of healing were performed. His travelling companion remarked, 'The Communists are terrified of supernatural power.' They certainly have reason to be in China. Members of the Communist Party or the People's Liberation Army are not permitted to be Christians. Yet many of these officials are witnessing and experiencing the supernatural power of God, and thus turning to Christ. The repercussions can often be far-reaching.

There is evidence from the Communist authorities themselves that healings are occurring with remarkable frequency, and right across the board. *The China Daily*, China's only newspaper in English, put out a report in September 1984 regarding Christian activity in Henan Province. It stated that 55% of Christians attended worship services because they hoped for healing. The report did not admit that actual healings were taking place, but such a statement would never have been made unless they were. Right from the start, the Three-Self Movement, which is required to keep Christianity in line with Party policy, has sought to discredit and discourage any emphasis on healing. This is in keeping with the liberal theology that characterizes the top echelon of the movement.

Despite this attitude, the healing power of God has been constantly breaking into the ranks of Party members. A special correspondent from Hong Kong records meeting 'a number of Party members' in the course of travelling inside China, 'some even holding fairly high positions, who had become Christians'. There was the Shanghai official whose daughter was healed of leukaemia in answer to prayer. This led the father to acknowledge Jesus Christ as Lord and Saviour. He is now witnessing for Christ although he has lost his high position, and been given the job of a janitor.

There was also a Party Committee Secretary suffering from cancer of the oesophagus, which, after four months, began to interfere seriously with his eating. The Government had given him a substantial sum of money, and the Production Brigade gave him 500 bricks for funeral preparations, and a grave site. His wife, who had seen many sick believe in Jesus and get well, encouraged her husband, 'Let us also believe in God.' He replied, 'Others may believe, but we cannot. I have persecuted many believers during the Cultural Revolution. Why should God cure me?'

However, his mother-in-law was a Christian, and she pointed out that Jesus did not come for the righteous, but for the sinners. So the Party Secretary believed. His mother-in-law then gave him a bowl of soup in Jesus' name and he drank it in faith. Within a few days he was eating normally and recovering rapidly.

While I was in Hong Kong a pastor told me of the case of the Party member who was taken sick. The Communists did not visit him, but the Christians did. They cleaned his house, made him meals and took care of him. It was their love in the first instance that opened his heart to the reality of Christ, and brought him to faith. Then they prayed for him and God healed him.

In a village in Shaanxi Province the Christians were in the middle of a prayer time when the Production Brigade leader and others burst in upon them. 'You are forbidden to believe in Jesus, and you are forbidden to pray,' he screeched. Many who were kneeling looked up in alarm, but a few minutes later it was the noisy intruders who had cause for alarm as they looked at their leader. His neck and mouth began to swell terribly and he was gasping for breath. 'You must repent and believe in Christ,' said the Christians. The man nodded his assent, began to pray, and immediately the swelling went down, and he began to praise God out loud.

So the Production Leader was changed from one who persecuted Christians to a dedicated disciple of Christ. Now he witnesses wherever he goes and has already led many people to Christ. The church was not only protected, but has been able to expand its ministry.

A young man in The People's Liberation Army was a sincere believer, although this was forbidden. When one of his fellows was taken seriously ill, he became deeply concerned that he would die without Christ and he shared the gospel with him. The man's condition continued to deteriorate, but-he took his friend's advice, turned to Christ and was almost instantly healed.

When his superiors found out, they tried to re-educate him in various ways, but he refused to give up his faith. His experience of healing had brought the awe of God upon him. The authorities concluded that they could do nothing with him, so they threw him out of the army. This would affect his education and employment for the rest of his life but he was too amazed at how the Lord had healed him to do anything else but believe. 'Today,' concludes a report, 'he serves the Lord with that sense of awe.'

A Christian wife on mainland China had been in ill-health for some time, latterly with pains in the liver. She kept on losing weight and the pain became unbearable. The doctor's verdict was cancer of the liver, for which he could do nothing. The Christian husband was in a state of depression when a letter came from Asian Outreach in Hong Kong, knowing nothing of the circumstances of the family. In the letter was a quotation from Ephesians 3. As the husband read the passage, these words lit up with a bright light, 'able to do immeasurably more than all we ask or imagine'.

Convinced that the disease was incurable, he had only been asking God to reduce the pain. 'I did not ask God to heal her. I dared not ask, I dared not hope.' He read the verses to the family and from then on they prayed every morning for God's healing. Within five days the pain stopped. His wife began to put on weight as though she was 'a balloon being inflated'. The doctor thought she was 'bloated', but found her muscles firm and strong. The family told the doctor that God had healed her. Though still weak at the time of writing, she was able to take care of her family and was confident that she would be fully restored.

The New Testament distinguishes between healings and miracles.[93] Like the one just recounted, many of these healings were in response to a prayer of faith, and had not been instantaneous. The promise of Jesus is, 'They will place their hands on sick people, and they will get well.'[94] This may or may not be instantaneous. Of course miracles are not confined to miracles of healing. When is a healing a miracle? When it is both instantaneous and manifest to all who behold. When people exclaim 'Wow!' then that is a miracle. There have been many instances where God's supernatural working has brought forth the 'Wow!' of wonder from the lips of those who witnessed it.

This story goes back to the early days of the Cultural Revolution. It is recounted by a young man whose family came from the hated landlord class, and who was healed before he knew the Lord. He described those terrible days for his family, while they waited for the inevitable: 'Since there was nowhere to flee we waited for death at home.' Tragedy hit his family in 1967 when the dormitory where he was living was struck by lightning. It set his clothes and hair on fire, and his body was seriously burned. People who came to put out the fire ignored him. Their only concern was to rescue the picture of Mao and his works. His mother, some distance away in the female dormitory was, as though compelled by some strange force, lifted out of bed. She rushed to his dormitory, and pushing aside the fireman she threw herself into the flames and rescued him.

Two days later he recovered consciousness in hospital. He was too weak even to lift a finger, and the burns on his body were festering, but the doctor told his mother, 'Your unit requires you to return and be reformed through labour. The boy cannot stay in hospital.' He also told her that because of the burns the nervous system was seriously damaged, and that he would be handicapped for life. Without a word his mother put him on a wooden cart and wheeled him home.

Three months later while his mother was at work, a golden light flooded into the room where the boy was lying, and he found he could sit up. The light seemed to be coming in from the mountainside, filling the whole cottage. He moved to get out of bed, and as his feet touched the floor he felt a warm current of 'electricity' running through his hands and feet. On her return, his mother was struck dumb with astonishment to see him walking about. 'Heaven has eyes,' she said, meaning heaven is merciful. When in 1969, amidst the tears of the family, he was sent to the countryside, his mother said to him, 'Child, go! Don't come back. You are different from the others. You are heaven-born and heaven-raised.'

He searched earnestly for God, and tried in vain to get hold of a Bible. Eventually God brought him to Hong Kong. Here he was put in touch with the Chinese Church Research Centre where he found Christ. Here is his testimony:

I firmly believe that God chose me to be a part of his people even before I was born. I am grateful to God for his enlightenment, his gifts and his selection. I thank God for his guidance one step at a time, for carrying me into his presence, and embracing me in his bosom at the right time. Because of him I have experienced a Spirit-filled baptism and am experiencing abundant Christian life.

Asian Outreach workers delivered a Bible to a young medical doctor in a small town of Central China. He recounted how a peasant woman who had a very bad accident was brought into hospital. A rock had crushed her chest, her rib cage was broken and some of her ribs had pierced her lungs. There was little he could do to save her life. As he placed the semi-conscious woman back on her bed, he heard her pray, 'Jesus, help me!'

Next day he was totally astonished to find the woman sitting up in bed eating a bowl of rice gruel. He had her X-rayed again, and was even more astonished to find that every single piece of her rib cage was perfectly healed! He told us, 'I have now personally seen the power of Jesus.' This man had never before seen a Bible or the inside of a church, but he was a firm believer in Christ.

There have also been cases of God's miraculous pro-vision. A village home in China held a special meeting to which many people travelled long distances. On their arrival the lady of the house served a hot meal, with food which the travellers had brought with them. Later on another group arrived. The lady knew they would be hungry, but she had no food left. She went into the kitchen to see what she could find, and there were pots with meat and vegetables in them. Supposing that the new arrivals had brought their own food, she served it up, and afterwards thanked them for bringing the food. 'What food?' they asked. 'We didn't bring any food. We ate all our provisions along the way.' They had experienced a mini-miracle of the 'five loaves and two small fishes'.

The authority Christ gives his people to deal with demonism is still a great door-opener to the gospel in China. Here is a recent testimony of a forty-five-year-old mother of four boys, whose husband was an engineer. They lived in that sparsely populated province, Qinghai, next to Tibet. After two boys, she wanted a girl, and prayed to Buddha that this third child she was carrying would be a daughter. To her great disappointment she had another boy. When this happened a fourth time she felt tricked, and lost control of herself. She left the baby on the ground to freeze to death, but her husband rescued him.

She became desperate when her husband was sent away on a course, and the devil seemed to take over. She wanted neither her husband nor her children, she just wanted to die. Once she tried to hang herself, but was discovered just in time. Her husband was recalled and he tried many famous doctors, all to no avail. His wife was like a mad woman. He decided to move his family back to Shandong.

By 1981 the husband and the four boys were caring for the demented woman all the time and all family joy had gone. He sought help from witches, and these cost him a lot of money. Early in 1983 a witch prophesied that his wife would get better as from the Spring Festival. The event came and went, and there was no improvement. The witch then admitted, 'My god is no longer effective. You had better try Jesus!' Previously some Christians had urged him to trust in Jesus, but he had not heeded. But now, in desperation, he was ready to heed the witch's advice.

Hearing of a meeting in the village, the husband, helped by his sons, balanced his wife on a bicycle and wheeled her there. On the way she tried to throw herself into a well screaming, 'After six years I can't bear any more!' The Christians were having Sunday worship. When they saw her they all united in prayer, and the demon was eventually cast out. Now they are a Christian family, and the wife testified, 'From then on I have never missed a meeting . . . my home is now full of joy as Jesus is the Head of our household.'

There have been prophetic words of warning given to Christians in times of danger. Three hundred pastors from different cities and towns had come together for a three day meeting. The authorities found out about it and sent secret police to investigate. As the pastors were praying, the word of the Lord came to one of them: 'The situation here is very dangerous and the police are coming to arrest you.' One by one the pastors dispersed, using different routes.

As soon as the last one was gone, the police came and the building was surrounded. They waited for the pastors to leave, so that they could arrest them. Eventually they became impatient and were ready to break down the door. To their surprise they found it ajar. The room was empty. The leader exclaimed in amazement more than in anger, 'These Christians are different. They know exactly what we are doing.'

In 1981 Christians in a certain city in Zhejiang Province persuaded a printing company to print 10,000 copies of *Streams in the Desert*,[95] a favourite devotional book in China. The firm did not realize that permission has always to be obtained from the authorities. When they found out, the printing was already completed, and they had only to cut the paper and bind the books. The police told them the books would be destroyed. Hearing this, the Christians began moving the materials from the factory to their homes to complete the project themselves.

Only a few were left when the police, learning what was happening, set a trap. They sent the army to surround the factory, waiting for the Christians to come that night, so that they could arrest them. But the Lord spoke to the believers and told them to stay away. The soldiers waited all night and next morning left before replacements arrived. At that very point the believers came and took the rest of the books away.

On finding there was not a single book left as evidence, the police were furious. They arrested the manager, fined him heavily, and put him in prison for ten days. When the believers visited him, he said, 'Do not feel bad. It is worth going to prison for ten days if one can get the message out. I will do it any time!' The incident was publicized as a news item—'Printing company accepts order for illegal propaganda material.'

These incidents are a small sample of the wonderful things that God is doing in China. The full story will probably never be told. We have reserved for the following chapter something of the remarkable way in which angelic ministry has been used to serve the body of Christ. Not only have they been used in deliverance and protection, but even in miracles of healing. It seems all of a piece with the spontaneous nature of the Spirit's working in that land.

Chapter Seventeen

HEAVEN'S AGENTS

*Are not all angels ministering spirits sent to serve
those who will inherit salvation?*

Hebrews 1:14

Angels are continually around us, and we are often the
unconscious recipients of their watchful care. As the
messengers of God's presence, they may bring words of
comfort, hope or counsel, often in situations of crisis or
at a strategic point in God's dealing with men. It is at
such times we become conscious of their presence, as
they break through that thin veil that separates the
visible from the invisible.

The early Christians were strong believers in the
ministry of angels. When Peter stood knocking at the
door of the home where Christians were praying for his
release from prison, a young woman named Rhoda
went to answer the knock. She recognized Peter's voice
and ran back to tell the praying saints that they could
get off their knees—the answer to their prayers was
knocking at the door. 'You're out of your mind,' they
told her. 'It must be his angel.'[96] They weren't so far
from the mark. His angel had only left him a short while
before, after getting him outside that prison gate!

174

As the conflict of the end time intensifies, and as persecution becomes the order of the day, we may expect to be hearing much more of angelic protection and provision. There is much that we have to learn about this neglected theme. Perhaps it is because the situation in China is in so many ways similar to New Testament times that angelic visitations are not uncommon.

During the Cultural Revolution a pastor in the very North of China was sentenced to be publicly executed in front of a firing squad because he refused to cease from preaching the gospel. While the squad was getting ready, he was asked if he had any last request. He replied that he would like to sing a song. Since it was a public execution permission was granted. He sang out in a booming voice, and as he sang the sky began to light up with the splendour of God's glory, and all the people that were gathered around heard what sounded like thousands of voices singing along with the pastor.

Shaken by the incident, the authorities decided to postpone the execution while an urgent telegram was sent off to Beijing for advice. Because of its nature, the telegram quickly found its way up the bureaucratic ladder until it reached Premier Zhou Enlai. Informed of the matter in detail, he sent back communication: 'This truly is no ordinary man. Release him and don't even bother him again.' The pastor was summarily released to do whatever he wanted, and he immediately began preaching, and as far as is known, he is still doing that today. Part of the song he sang, translated into English reads:

> Lord, I love you!
> My heart seeks after you.
> Because of you I forsake everything,
> And despise wealth and fame.

Paul Kauffman tells of a young Christian sent from his home town to work in a commune hundreds of miles away in the Island of Hainan. Because of his isolation, he had become luke-warm in his faith. One night when he was asleep in the dormitory with his fellow workers, a typhoon hit the island. It is not uncommon for this to happen and to bring gales of up to 100 miles per hour.

In the midst of the howling storm he was startled by someone calling his name outside the dormitory. He sat up in bed, but was reluctant to go out, because of the danger. Finally, the voice was so insistent that he went out. At that moment the building collapsed behind him. Several were killed and all were injured. As a result of this experience, this young man found a boldness in witnessing that he had never had before. More than 200 people came to Christ in the following eighteen months.[97]

In 1975 there was a church that used to hold retreats and training classes for young converts in the nearby mountains. They were having a baptismal service for 100 converts when militia men arrived to prevent the baptisms. However, they saw soldiers surrounding the Christians, and so withdrew their detachment in the belief that the army had the matter in hand. The only soldiers were from the heavenly army, and so the baptismal service proceeded without interference.

In conversation with representatives of *Open Doors* Brother Nui of China was asked what the Christians did at their Sunday evening meetings since there were few Bibles, fewer songbooks and no Bible teacher. He said that they came together to praise God for what he had done, and then give several testimonies of the wonderful things that God was doing.

Among the events he recounted was that of a small boy who went out with his grandmother to the fields.

He was killed when he was run over by a heavily loaded cart. The grandmother was overwhelmed with fear and buried the boy herself. Afraid to tell her daughter what had happened, she said that the child had wandered off in the streets. The grief-stricken family was having dinner when the little boy walked into the home. He explained that a man in white had lifted him from the ground, brushed off the dirt from his clothes and face, and told him to go back home.

Mr Huang was a worshipper of Buddha. His health began to deteriorate until he could not keep any food down. The doctor diagnosed cancer of the liver in the terminal stage, and said there was nothing that could be done for him. So he returned to his native village to await death. While there he heard about a doctor in the town, and decided to get a second opinion. This doctor who was a Christian (and accompanied the man as he gave this testimony) confirmed that the diagnosis was correct and that the illness was incurable.

He then told the man that there was no medicine that could prolong his life, but that if he would believe in Jesus Christ, he could have eternal life. The gospel was explained to him and he was urged to believe on the Lord Jesus Christ. The doctor also explained that Jesus had the power to heal any sickness if that were his will.

'But whether Jesus heals you or not is not important,' said the doctor. 'What is important is that you have eternal life.'

Mr Huang said 'I want to believe in Jesus.' They knelt in his office as Mr Huang became a new person in Christ.

Returning home he told his wife of his faith in Christ and asked her to remove all the idols from the house and burn them. She did this, but Mr Huang's condition deteriorated rapidly. Every night he and his wife knelt to pray. He thanked the Lord that whatever happened to him physically, he now had eternal life. He was gripped by terrible pain, and became so weak that the family commenced preparations for his funeral. The coffin was purchased and the grave dug on the hillside.

One night a man in a white robe appeared to him in his sleep. He was holding a knife. Fearing his intentions, Mr Huang struggled with the man in white, but he prevailed and touched Mr Huang with the knife. Next morning he awoke at eight o'clock, hungry for the first time in many days. After eating a nourishing bowl of soup, he fell asleep.

When he woke he clearly saw two men in white robes standing by his bed. They said, 'You have been healed.' He reached down and found all of his swelling gone. Being extremely hungry, he ate a hearty meal. When his brother came to pay him a visit, he was amazed to see him sitting up. He testified to his brother that Jesus had touched him during the night and he was completely healed.

From Zhejiang, reputed to be a province with a very large number of Christians, comes this story of a village woman with a brain tumour. For nine years she had tried to find a cure, spending all her money in vain. She then gave up all hope and resigned herself to die.

One day, lying on her bed alone in the house, she saw three people in white robes enter her room. One of them asked her, 'Do you want to be healed?'

A little surprised, she replied, 'Are you a doctor? Yes, I want to be healed.'

The man in white came near and stroked her head where the tumour was. She felt fluid coming out of her head and a lump being removed. The man then seemed to close up the opening with a few quick movements of his fingers. She felt instantly relieved. She then asked, 'What is your name, doctor?'

The man in white answered, 'Jesus. You may find me in the nearest town.' Then he disappeared.

She told the family when they returned in the evening about the doctor who gave her free treatment. They paid no attention to her, thinking she was delirious. But she grew stronger every day; her brain tumour was gone. Then she set out for the neighbouring town to find the doctor who had healed her, in order to thank him.

'Is there a doctor here by the name of Jesus?' The woman she addressed was a Christian, who thought for a second, and then decided to take the enquirer to her home where Christians gathered to worship. She told her story. The Christians were not surprised to hear of her healing as it is so common in rural China. But she was awestruck when they told her who Jesus was. They preached repentance and salvation to her and she went home with Jesus in her heart.

Shortly after, her whole family came to Christ. Her testimony quickly spread in her village and many people wanted to believe in Jesus. She fetched a more mature Christian from the town, and as a result many people came to the Lord.

There was a very poor Christian couple who made their living hauling stones and logs on wooden hand-carts. They were straining to get a heavy load of stones up a hill. When they reached the top, the wife ran round to the front to steady the cart on the reverse slope. She tripped and fell, and the cart passed over her body, crushing her bones. Local doctors said she would have to go to a larger hospital for major surgery, but this was far more than the couple could afford.

On the fourth night in hospital the drugs were still giving her no relief from her excessive pain. As she waited on the Lord, she decided to stop all the pain killers, and trust God for healing. That night two 'strangers' visited her. They lifted her by the shoulders and pressed down on her pelvic bone. She said it was as though 'boiling water' was passing through her body from head to foot. When she awakened next morning she kept saying, 'Thank you, Lord! Praise the Lord!'

'What's the matter?' asked the lady in the next bed.

'My body is well again,' she replied. 'The angels have operated on my bones.'

When the doctors came to examine her, she told them what had happened. They were amazed to find that her bones were perfect, and she was allowed to check out of the hospital at noon that day.

A few days later she went to the market and bought some fruit and candies. Then she stood by the road and stopped people as they passed to tell them her testimony of God's healing power. To each who would listen, she gave some fruit and candy—her thank offering![98]

For several generations, Dr Wang's family had lived in the two-storey house surrounding a local courtyard. Despite misgivings at the time of the Revolution, he had worked hard to serve the people. When the Cultural Revolution struck, old Dr Wang, trained in western medicine and known to be a Christian, was one of the first targets for persecution. No one quite knows what they did to him, for he never spoke about his sufferings, but Dr Wang could no longer walk. He was confined to his bed in an upstairs room, and was cared for by his family.

One night, as Dr Wang's daughter-in-law lay awake unable to sleep, she heard the creaking sound of the great wooden gate into the courtyard. Springing up, she ran to the narrow veranda to see a white clad figure enter the house. She went downstairs to investigate, but no one was there, except family members fast asleep.

Meanwhile, in the little room upstairs, old Dr Wang

stirred in his sleep. A bright light shone down upon him and his eyes opened to a vision of the Lord Jesus standing beside the bed. 'Son,' he heard Jesus say. 'Get up and walk!'

'I cannot walk,' he replied with surprise. So Jesus reached out his hands and lifted him up.

'Do you believe in me?' Jesus asked.

'I do, I do, Lord!' he answered.

'If you believe in me,' Jesus said. 'Get up and walk.'

Without hesitation, the old man obeyed. He rose from his bed and began walking. Then he began to laugh out loud with joy, and it seemed the Lord laughed with him. It was two-thirty in the morning and the laughter woke his nephew who slept in the same room. He thought his uncle had gone out of his mind, and rushed to support him lest he fall.

In another room, Dr Wang's eldest son was awakened by the commotion. He jumped up and was shocked to see his father standing by his bed laughing. He too thought the old man had gone mad. He was about to clutch him when his father said very firmly, 'Keep your hands off me! I am not out of my mind. The Lord Jesus came to this room! He has healed me!'

With these words he walked down the steep stairway to the ground floor, turned round and smiled up at his frightened family. Then he began walking up again with steady steps. As he reached the top, the joy of the family knew no bounds. Their excitement woke up everyone in the household.

Such good news could not wait till morning. The entire family trooped over to the second son's home in another street. 'Look! Grandpa is walking!' cried the youngest son, as one by one the startled family members joined the excited group. Laughing and rejoicing, they gave thanks to God together.

Dr Wang wanted to continue to the meeting place of the believers, but his sons persuaded him to wait till morning. At dawn the family went to the astonished pastor and then to other relatives. They met his young niece on her way to work. She stared open-mouthed to see him walking. Hearing what had happened she began praising the Lord, saying, 'Blessed be our God! He is so wonderful!'

The following Sunday the house where the believers gathered for worship was crowded out. People stood in the courtyard and looked in through the windows. Others filled the alleyway. All eyes were on old Dr Wang who was moving from room to room greeting the Christians. To a hushed company he told his amazing story. Questions flew, and he answered them one by one.

'Dr Wang, can you jump?' asked the Pastor.

'Can I jump? Of course I can!' said the old man, and with that he began to jump up and down for all to see.

Dr Wang now travels far and wide on his bicycle telling all who will listen about the power of Jesus. People are not only listening, they are calling upon the name of the Lord and being saved.

Many will want to know whether these independent house churches in China are 'charismatic'? That really depends on what you mean by 'charismatic'. If you are asking, 'Are these Christians wide open to the in-filling and gifts of the Holy Spirit? Do they expect God to do today what he did in Bible times? Do they view such things as normal, when they do occur?' the answer would almost certainly be yes to all these questions. When it comes to healing there is surely more faith among the house churches of China than there is amongst the majority of believers in the West who call themselves pentecostal or charismatic.

If, however, you mean, 'Is there clear teaching on the baptism in the Holy Spirit and the spiritual gifts? Is there real freedom in praise and worship? Does the exercise of tongues, interpretation of tongues and prophecy feature in their meetings?' The answer would largely be no. Of course one is generalizing, and there will be numerous exceptions to these two answers.

There is almost universal acceptance of the fact that God heals today. They believe in the validity of the gifts and manifestations of the Spirit, and are open to them but there's probably little emphasis on earnestly desiring them, as Paul exhorts us to do, and little biblical teaching on their proper exercise in the church.

What is God wanting to say to us through this aspect of his working in China? In a nation which is largely free from the influence of the West, and where there is no strong 'lobby' for or against supernatural manifestations, God is none-the-less moving spontaneously in this way. What does that say to us? Why healings are featuring so prominently in this is surely because they are mightily effective in this current phase of evangelistic growth. Do we not desperately need such growth in our own land?

The other lesson is the openness of the Chinese believers, and the simplicity of their faith. It is true that they have had little teaching. In the mercy of God, no one has been around to warn them that 'these things' were confined to primitive Christianity, and that God does not work in these ways today and that therefore any such manifestations are counterfeit. Q.E.D! Thus when God began to work in such ways they welcomed such working with great gladness.

We need to come out of our pose of negativism or of neutrality, if we have adopted such. We need to begin to call on the Lord, as the early church did—and as the church in China is now doing—that God would stretch forth his hand to heal and that signs and wonders may be done.

A time must surely come in China when this present phase of phenomenal growth gives way to one of consolidation. Then I believe God will lead those churches to seek the gifts that are specially given for edification. Scriptures will light up to them, such as: 'Eagerly desire spiritual gifts, especially the gift of prophecy';[99] and 'Since you are eager to have spiritual gifts, try to excel in gifts that build up the church.'[100] Not only gifts of teaching and exhortation, but also the public use of tongues in conjunction with interpretation, the gift of prophecy and others come into this category.[101] One thing is certain, God will not withhold any good gift that is needed for the maturing of his church in China.

Chapter Eighteen

HOUSE CHURCHES EAST AND WEST

You too are being built together to become a dwelling in which God lives by his Spirit.

Ephesians 2:22

The term 'house churches' in Britain is a confusing misnomer. A misnomer because many of them have outgrown homes and moved to larger premises. In any case, they never put any importance on the nature of the meeting-place. Confusing, because in the way they now use homes they are no different from many historic churches, which break down into home groups midweek, while still holding Sunday services in the church building.

In their human origins the house churches in China and the West have no connection whatsoever. That makes their similarities, which we are now to consider, all the more significant. A builder friend of mine put his house, built by himself, on the market. He could tell that the man who came to view it was in the construction business by the things he spotted and the remarks that he made. When this prospective purchaser came for a second look, he said, 'I can pick out your houses all over the town.' It was not that they were all the same, but that they had distinctive features. There is great variety and flexibility in New Testament churches, but there are also distinctive features that tell us that the 'architect and builder is God'.

There is always a *timing for God's working*. This provides an interesting connection between East and West. It may not be possible to pinpoint the beginning of the house churches in China as we now know them, for there were cottage meetings before the Communists took over, and homes were used in the early years of their regime. The 'birth' or breaking out of the movement came with the end of the Cultural Revolution. So the germination was taking place during those dark days (1966–1978) when the Christian church was underground. The small beginnings of the house churches in Britain belong to the same period. Conferences were held, hearts were stirred, but in 1972 there was a knitting together of a handful of men who shared the same vision.

God told that group of men that they were not to view themselves in any way above their brothers because of what he was showing them. They were but a 'sample', and what he was doing with them he would do with others all over the world. It was some two years later that they discovered that God had moved similarly and at the same time with a group of men in the USA. Since then other individuals and groups, whose hearts were similarly stirred by the Holy Spirit, and who had found a new relationship together, have come to light. The timings of God are significant.

In comparing East with West, it is immediately obvious that the way God worked in China to bring to birth the kind of churches he was wanting, was utterly different than in, say, Britain and the USA. In China it was mainly through the iron fist of Communism and the pressure of circumstances; here in the West, it was more by revelation and conviction—but the same architect and builder was at work in each.

There was first of all a *return to simplicity*. God used the Communists, as we have seen, to break down the denominational structures of the church in China. Their idea was to force believers into the common mould of the Three-Self Patriotic Movement. Many Christians refused to be so forced. Families began to meet in their homes for prayer and Bible study. Others began to find one another in a new relationship. Gone was the old western denominational wineskin, although much of the old form was being resurrected in the Three-Self movement.

Like the churches of the New Testament, the only structure these persecuted believers now had was one of great simplicity. It was the structure that comes when heart is knitted with heart, and a unity is formed by the action of the Holy Spirit. They discovered that this kind of joining together *is* the house of God, the place where God is pleased to dwell by his Spirit.

For us in the West it was a 'simplicity' that we began to see and to hunger for. It was not something that just happened. It was not something we discovered, but that God revealed to our seeking hearts. Though we did not have to endure beatings and imprisonment, that does not mean that obedience to the heavenly vision was without price. It nearly always involves misunderstanding, criticism, and reproach.

Then there was the bringing forth of an *anointed leadership*. Slowly but surely the Communists increased their stranglehold on the church. If leaders did not readily co-operate by joining the Three-Self, they were subjected to struggle sessions and every other conceivable kind of pressure. Some cracked; others found themselves sentenced to many years in prison. Meanwhile, God was quietly at work in many a home group, preparing and training a new generation of leaders for a new day that was to dawn.

Outside the Three-Self movement there was now no denominational hierarchy, no synods, boards or councils, to choose and appoint new leaders. They were being thrown up by the situation, just as they were in the early church. It was not difficult for the maturer saints to recognize the ones on whom the anointing of the Spirit was resting. A man's qualification was not that he had been selected by a 'board' or had a diploma from some seminary, but that he knew God and had been chosen, called and gifted by God for the job he was doing.

It may not be possible at this stage to identify all the gifts that God is bestowing on his people in China. Much is still in its formative stage. But this much is clear, he is raising up many teachers, pastors, evangelists and those used in healing. In answer to prayer, he will surely provide all that his church needs for its future development.

This is the basis on which leadership is recognized in the many churches with which I am familiar in the West. There are those with apostolic and prophetic gifts whom God uses to spot, train and encourage emerging leaders. I do not know whether that is yet happening in China. Certainly it has produced in the past men of apostolic gift. But whether East or West, the indispensable qualification for leadership is knowing God and the anointing of his Spirit.

Then there is *congregational participation*. Paul wrote to the Corinthians: 'When you come together, everyone

has a hymn, or a word of instruction, a revelation....'[102]
This way of proceeding does not go well with the formal
church setting, but is a natural way of operating in a
family setting, and in church the Chinese Christians
have rediscovered 'family'. The many-membered body
has found itself, and its members are functioning. This
was one of the open secrets of the rapid development
and maturing of the believers in New Testament times.
This is now happening in China.

Back in the West we have come to recognize the
importance of this principle out of our understanding of
'the body of Christ', and because of God bestowing
upon the body gifts of the Holy Spirit. Such participation
is often called 'body ministry'. Whatever is the point of
'the manifestation of the Spirit' being given to each one
in the body,[103] if only the man at the front is really free
to exercise his gift? How quickly the believers develop
and mature when they learn to step out in faith and
participate by giving thanks, praying, testifying or
exercising a spiritual gift. A body functioning in this
way is also fertile ground for raising up new leadership.

In the previous two chapters we have spoken of the
Chinese Christians' *openness to the Holy Spirit and to his
supernatural manifestations*. For this reason one would
expect them to be at home in the house churches of the
West, but not so comfortable with those churches that
insist that such things are not for today. I recall a visit to
North Thailand years ago. Many among the hill tribes
had found Christ, and churches had been established.
A serious rift had occurred between these believers and
the missionary organization working in the area, because
of the mission policy to discourage any manifestations
of the Spirit. The national believers could not understand the missionaries' attitude towards something
which was so clearly scriptural and which had brought

them such blessing.

Circumstances have providentially prevented the Chinese believers from thinking in terms of '*consecrated buildings*'. We have seen that they meet in private homes, warehouses, even in business premises, courtyards or in the open air. Very occasionally, in rural areas, they may be able to secure a building for worship. But often they are compelled to move from home to home. This has been a continual reminder that the church is not the building, and 'the sanctuary' is not the bricks and mortar. As the old hymn put it—

> Where e'er they seek thee thou art found,
> And every place is hallowed ground.

This is very much the view that shapes the thinking of the New Testament churches in the West. They are not against the procuring of buildings as meeting places, but they believe that the expenditure of vast sums of money on church property is not only a misapplication of the resources entrusted to them, but a serious hindrance to swift growth. Elaborate and costly buildings put the emphasis on the wrong thing. It does not seem to have considered the end-time shaking predicted in Scripture.[104] What would happen to such buildings in a time of protracted persecution? The fact that the Communists have taken over missionary schools, hospitals and church buildings for secular purposes must make us wonder whether the large sums involved could have been far more wisely spent.

Finally, these churches in East and West have a similar *attitude to spiritual mixture* in the professing church. They do not have to cope with quite the same denominational hotch-potch that we face in the West. In China it is all in one bag—the Three-Self Patriotic Movement. The house church leaders know full well that the Religious Affairs Bureau of the Communist Government, which is entirely political, calls the tune, and the Three-Self has to comply. To most house church leaders this involves denying the lordship of Christ over his church, and though they acknowledge there are good men there, they will not join, for that would be compromise.

Many church leaders, even evangelicals, outside China have been beguiled by the smooth words of Bishop Ding and his colleagues, who head up the Three-Self and its sister organization, the China Christian Council. They travel overseas, endeavouring to impress the outside world that China has human rights and religious freedom. This is a travesty of truth when you know that pastors from the house churches are still being arrested, their churches closed down, and their flocks told that they must now worship in the newly opened Three-Self churches. 'There is no religious freedom,' says Paul Kauffman. 'Communism cannot permit freedom. It can and does permit some practice of religion. This is a very important distinction. All religion is carefully controlled by the State.' Christians are told where they are to worship, who is allowed to preach, the parish to which he is confined and what may be printed and published.

No Bibles or Christian literature are allowed to be printed without permission of the Religious Affairs Bureau. Young people do not have religious freedom. It is an offence to try to influence them with the gospel. Three-Self Bibles in the past have been in the traditional script which is no longer taught in the schools. The authorities do not want young people to read and believe. These are some of the reasons why so many of the leaders of the unofficial churches take a strong stand, and refuse to compromise with the official church, though in towns and cities they are under increasing pressure to do so.

In the West, though the situation is completely different, house churches generally take a radical stance over denominational mixture. This may have caused some to develop an exclusive posture but most have warm relationships with those in traditional and free church settings. But they do not allow this to weaken their convictions with regard to New Testament principles that they have embraced. They do not want to belong to an 'official church' whatever the immediate advantages may appear to be, any more than their brothers and sisters in China. Their convictions about the church make them radical.

So we have looked at seven significant characteristics of house churches, East and West. But how important are they? Ours is a practical God, as well as a God of principle. When we adopt New Testament ways, we are also being pragmatic. God's ways work best. He has taken every contingency into consideration.

Let us look at two aspects of their practical importance. First, denominational Christianity, with its central organization and complex machinery is brittle rather than flexible, and where the ruling authority is antagonistic, it is easily brought under government control—as in China. It can then be weakened and, when it has served its purpose, destroyed. That is the Communist theory. The New Testament church structure is simple and flexible, designed to survive and even flourish in times of persecution.

'The more imposing the edifice, the more easily it is found by the gunner. The more obvious and obtrusive an organisation, the more readily it is attacked and ruined.'[105] We can see the significance of this in China, but we are very foolish and short-sighted if we suppose that this could never overtake us in the West. As we have said before, the predictions of Scripture are clear. As the end time conflict intensifies, and persecution will become much more general: 'He is worse prepared who is least prepared for the worst.'

Second, the simplicity of New Testament churches means that they are geared for mission and for growth. The Chinese house churches have been divested of surplus baggage. Their resources are channelled into evangelism and shepherding. Their understanding of community gives them a sense of belonging and of cohesion. Their emphasis on 'the body' encourages everyone to participate. Non-functioning members are a small minority. Each feels he has a part to play, so there is a high deployment of the church's potential.

It must be admitted that in former years much of the growth of the house churches came through discontented believers who found in the new churches the kind of fellowship that they were looking for. This has brought from some disgruntled pastors the rather foolish charge of 'sheep stealing'. The two-legged variety are not stolen! If they move, they move of their own volition. I have yet to come across any church that turns away hungry sheep looking for fresh grass and still waters.

Now the situation is rapidly changing. A growing number joining the house churches are new converts with no church background. One wishes they were all like that—they are so much easier to shepherd! We are now in a situation where it is New Testament churches, whether East or West, with a structure geared for mission, that are by and large the fastest growing churches of the twentieth century.

The Great Wall of China.

Chapter Nineteen

A CRY FOR HELP

*He has delivered us from such a deadly peril, and
he will deliver us. On him we have set our hope
that he will continue to deliver us, as you help us
by your prayers.*

2 Corinthians 1:10–11

As I have been writing, my mind has travelled back to
my first visit to New Zealand in 1963. A number had
been stirred at that time to pray for the outpouring of
the Holy Spirit. In Auckland I met some godly women
who were true intercessors. 'Has God shown you anything about China?' one of them asked me.

'No,' I replied.

'Well, he has shown us,' came the reply, 'that that
great land, now so tightly closed, will one day open right
up to the gospel—and we are praying for that to happen.'
At that point China's darkest hour, the great Cultural
Revolution, was still future. But God heard the prayers
of many saints throughout the world, and delivered his
people 'from such a deadly peril'.

In 1975 China was again approaching a crucial era,
which was destined to set the whole nation on a new
course. A worldwide prayer movement was set on foot,

which found expression in Britain during the following two years in the 'China—too hard for God?' campaign. This set hundreds of British Christians praying. That year of 1976 witnessed the death of Mao Zedong, as well as the arrest and imprisonment of the Gang of Four, who had planned to seize power and keep the country on a leftist course. The more liberal policies that followed opened the way for this great movement of the Spirit. The hopes of the Chinese Christians that God would 'continue to deliver' were fulfilled through the help of many prayers.

There are numerous ways in which we can play a part in what God is now doing in China: taking in Bibles and Christian literature, supporting ministries into China, especially radio broadcasts, befriending Chinese students in our universities, with a view to witnessing to them, etc. But this chapter will try to give some guidelines on the question of prayer help, as that is part of God's commission in the writing of this book.

There has been much publicity about the shortage of Bibles and Christian literature, especially in the rural areas. Although it is most important that we pray and support those who are seeking to meet this need, an even greater need is that of *anointed leadership*. The church of the first century grew and flourished without the general availability of Scriptures, but it could not have happened without leadership. The need of Bibles and literature is being met, although there is lots more to be done, but the immediate need can be relieved with the raising up of mature leadership.

We need to pray for the ministries of 'apostles, prophets, evangelists, pastors and teachers',[106] which Paul reminds us are the gifts of the ascended Christ to his body. China has had men of apostolic calibre in the past, like Pastor Hsi and Watchman Nee, who have been true church planters. But they are needed more than ever today to shape and structure the Chinese church of the future. There is also the need of prophets, men with prophetic vision and insight, who will help guide the church through the difficult days that lie ahead.

God is already raising up evangelists, shepherds and teachers, but the need for these is still great. As an elderly pastor put it: 'Before the Communists came, I remember that shepherds were searching for sheep. But now, all over China, it is the sheep who are searching for shepherds!' These gifts are bestowed in response to prayer. The answer lies within the scope and ministry of the intercessor.

As we have read these pages, have we heard God speak to us through the church in China? Have we recognized that this was 'a now word' to us? The church in China, as God's people everywhere, is prophetic, that is, they have 'a now word' for their day and generation. We need to pray that they may come in to a fuller understanding of their destiny in God, and of their prophetic calling, not only to Communist China, but to the whole world.

When God first spoke to me about writing this book, and then opened the way for me to visit China, I prayed that he would give me a travelling companion, preferably Chinese, but at least fluent in Mandarin, who would take me in and provide the openings. I had hoped for introductions to house church leaders, and perhaps to see for myself a house church in action. God did not fulfil these desires, at least not on that first trip. Instead it proved to be the loneliest trip I have ever made in thirty-five years of itinerant ministry.

I had flown into Shanghai where I hoped to be joined by an American brother and a party of Chinese from

Hong Kong. My American friend at first failed to locate me. In the guest house, where I was staying, I dined in solitary grandeur. The authorities were, at that time, careful to ensure that foreign visitors had as little contact as possible with the Chinese. I will never forget taking a taxi to a department store in the heart of Shanghai. It was a few days before the Chinese New Year. I found myself literally propelled into the store by the shoving, milling crowd. It was just like being outside Wembley after the cup final. I had never seen such crowds. Back on the streets, I could not get a taxi. No one had told me you have to go to special pick-up points, so for nearly an hour I walked the streets of Shanghai.

I was cold. An injured ankle began to ache. I did not know where to go. I could not communicate. I looked in vain for a western face. During that hour a thousand pairs of Chinese eyes must have surveyed me with curiosity. Surely some of these people must be Christians, I thought. I had been told there were one million in Shanghai. A great longing swept over me just to grip one believer's hand, just to exchange a smile of greeting, just to say that word that every Christian knows, whatever his language—'Hallelujah'. But there was no way we could find each other. I had never experienced such a feeling of utter helplessness and desolation. Had I come all the way to China for this?

That night in my room, my Father spoke to me. 'I have given you today for a few minutes a tiny taste of what thousands of my children continually experience in China. They know what it is to feel cut off, even from their fellow Chinese. When it comes to fellowship, they speak another language, belong to another culture. They are 'aliens and strangers' to the world, and likewise the world to them. Some of them are in prison, for the sake of my name. Others are in labour camps, hundreds of miles from home, loved ones and Christian fellowship. I gave you this experience that you might begin to identify with them, pray for them and encourage others to pray.'

A young Christian who reached Hong Kong testified to how the hymn 'No, never alone' had been a tower of strength to her. Reared in a Christian home, she gave her life to Christ at eleven. She went to study at a university thousands of miles from her home town. And at university they used to hold criticism meetings. Because she was a Christian they would put her in the circle and cross-examine her. Then one of the group would read a prepared speech. When they grew tired of this, they would send her away until they wanted to repeat the process. She recalled, 'I was very much alone at that time. No one wanted to be seen talking to me. Although living on campus, I ate alone and studied alone.'

One evening she was feeling very lonely and heavy-laden. Walking up a nearby mountain the song came to her mind, 'No, never alone'. She started singing the song softly, and then louder and louder, till joy filled her and overwhelmed her. She knew that the Lord was with her.

After graduation she was assigned to a factory job in the bitterly cold climate of Manchuria. Again, she was a long way from home. They shifted her from factory to factory, giving her the dirtiest and most exhausting work, involving long hours—just because she was a Christian. 'My family would never have recognized this dirty factory worker.' Many of her colleagues contracted occupational diseases, but God kept her healthy. In the university they had criticized her, but in the factory her treatment was far worse. Here she was condemned as an anti-revolutionary. But again and again she was comforted by the song 'No, never alone'.[107]

The word of God exhorts us not only to pray for, but to identify with all those who suffer for their Christian faith.

'Remember those in prison as if you were their fellow-prisoners, and those who are ill-treated as if you your-selves were suffering.'[108] Surely it has been the power of prayer that has brought such Christians through their ordeals, and has even 'served to advance the gospel'.[109]

A group of itinerant preachers from Central China who met for a work conference, put out a number of prayer requests, one of which was:

Please pray for our imprisoned brothers and sisters. Lord, give them strength to match their days. Increase their inner strength and let it suffer no loss. Manifest the power of your outstretched arm of deliverance, and perform a miracle in setting free the imprisoned and leading them home. Shorten the terms of those who are sentenced to long terms, so that they will have more time to do your work.[110]

As political and economic considerations continue to compel the Chinese Communist Party to adopt a 'softly softly' policy towards Christianity, to give the outside world the impression of religious tolerance, their efforts to force the house churches into the Three-Self Move-ment, and so under control, are almost certain to inten-sify. This is an area of great danger for the future of the church in China. Hence those same itinerant preachers included this further prayer request:

Ask the Lord to bind heresies and expose the Big Harlot's nakedness, so that people will understand and escape from her snares. (A note here explains that the Big Harlot is the TSPM. The house church leaders are comparing the TSPM to the Israelites who committed fornication with the Moabites in Numbers 25:1–9.)

We need to pray that house church leaders will see the issues very clearly as far as the Three-Self churches are concerned, take their lead from God and refuse to compromise, rather than being influenced by leaders within the Three-Self, godly men though some of them may be.

We are commanded to pray for our rulers, 'that we may live peaceful and quiet lives in all godliness and holiness'.[111] For God to answer such a prayer for China will not necessarily mean the overthrow of the Communist regime, or that it will cease to persecute the church. But it would mean that the country would be saved from the breakdown of law and order such as accompanied the Cultural Revolution, when all Christian activity virtually ceased. As the scripture goes on to explain, the purpose of such prayer is to facilitate the spread of the gospel. This came to halt in the Cultural Revolution, but burst into life when that period ended.

If we feel led to pray for the total destruction of the Bamboo Curtain, and that China will join the ranks of the free world, we need to be very sure that this is God's will for this time. If the Communist authorities seem reluctant to open the door any wider than is economically necessary to the 'unacceptable face of capitalism', and to so much decadence that goes along with western culture, who can blame them? Of course we know there are other reasons. How tragic if China were suddenly inundated with western denominationalism, with every conceivable brand of Christian ministry and organization, teaching and emphasis, all jostling to get on the China Church bandwagon? What a good thing that control of the Bamboo Curtain is not left in our hands.

Many with a deep concern for the future of the Chinese church would echo the fear of Tony Lambert of Christian Communications when he says:

The real danger is that Western Christians, with more zeal than knowledge, will again seek to re-impose denominational structures and cultural attitudes which will undo all that has been accomplished in the providence of God over the last thirty years.

Equally pertinent are the words of veteran missionary to China, Paul Kauffman:

> We must recognize the cultural maturing of China's church and not permit our culture to again infiltrate and thus deform a church that has, at great price, become truly indigenous.[112]

To help those who may wish to start praying intelligently for the church in China, here is a list of suggested prayer points, including those we have already mentioned:

1. For those in prison or labour camp who are suffering for Jesus' sake. For those who have been arrested and are awaiting trial, and for all under threat of this. For those who are enduring loneliness for Christ's sake.

2. For those at home suffering because loved ones, and perhaps the bread winner, have been arrested. That they may know God's comfort, protection and supply.

3. For evangelists and itinerant preachers who are the 'Christian fugitives' of China, and who pay a great price to fulfil their ministry.

4. For leaders who are under pressure to compromise and lose their liberty in Christ by joining the TSPM, that they may stand firm, and that the Christians may stand with them.

5. That there may not be animosity between believers of the house churches and those in the Three-Self. That believers in the house churches may be able to recognize and receive their brothers and sisters in the Three-Self, while rejecting the system that they have joined.

6. For the raising up of new leaders—for apostles, prophets, evangelists, shepherds and teachers, and all those whom God is calling to preach and to witness.

7. That the church as a whole will be nourished and grow strong, knowing its prophetic calling and destiny.

8. That God will overrule the decisions of the Communist authorities so as to grant peace in the land, that the gospel may be fully proclaimed. That God will have the Bamboo Curtain under his control, to facilitate his purpose for his church in China.

9. For the supply of Bibles and Christian literature to meet the growing need, and that Christians taking these into China will act wisely and judiciously.

10. For those whose ministry is preparing and beaming radio broadcasts into China, whether evangelistic, Bible teaching or leadership material.

11. For those preparing printed teaching materials and Bible study courses for Christians in mainland China.

12. For Chinese students who have gone to study at western universities, that Christians may befriend them and lead them to Christ.

13. For the growing number of Christians from the West who are regularly going into China, whether teachers, business men, technicians or students, that the pressures to which they are subjected may not dull their witness for Christ.

14. For the church in Hong Kong, at present ill-prepared for the Communist takeover in 1997, that it may be cleansed and renewed, united and dedicated for the testings that must lie ahead.

Chapter Twenty

THE WAKING GIANT

Now to him who is able to do immeasurably more than all we ask or imagine, according to his power that is at work within us . . .

Ephesians 3:20

As a land, China is possessed of immense natural resources and almost unlimited manpower. As a people, the Chinese have been endowed with fertile minds and outstanding natural abilities. Isolated for millennia by a sense of their self-sufficiency and even racial superiority, the people of 'the middle country' are at last relating with the big outside world. What does the future hold for them?

Two hundred years ago someone asked Napoleon for his views on China. 'China?' replied the Emperor. 'There lies a sleeping giant. Let him sleep, for when he wakes he will move the world.'

On an October morning in 1949, in front of 'The Forbidden City' in the heart of Beijing (Peking) Chairman Mao Zedong gave notice to the world that 'the sleeping giant' had not only wakened, but had got to his feet: 'The Chinese people have stood up!'

Across the nation the words were taken up by jubilant

young Communists. 'Yes,' they cried, 'the Chinese people have stood up at last!'

That was more than thirty-five years ago. It has been an uphill struggle, and not without some disastrous setbacks, but now China can no longer be viewed as a Third World country, struggling for survival. She has become a member of the United Nations. She has joined 'the nuclear club'. She is even being described as 'a candidate super-power'. Arnold Toynbee, that perceptive historian, once said, 'The twenty-first century will belong to China.' Some with an eye on God's prophetic clock, might ask, 'Will there be a twenty-first century?' In the world scene events are taking place with frightening rapidity. The sands of time are running out.

Of far greater significance to us than any political or economic awakening of the Chinese Giant is the great spiritual awakening that has been the central theme of this book. Millions are now giving the 'thumbs down' to the atheistic philosophy of Marxism, and turning their faces towards Christ. Just how many of these are truly regenerated it may be difficult to say, but there is no mistaking the trend, and the Communists can do nothing about it. Said Jonathan Chao of the Chinese Church Research Centre:

> After ten years of China study and five years of research into the church in China, I have come to the conclusion that in fifteen to twenty years China will become the greatest harvest field in the history of mankind.

That is a thrilling prospect, but it has never been in the heart of Chinese believers to be the nation that is always at the receiving end of God's grace. There has always been the burning desire to reach out to others. China has had much to give. Who can measure the

influence of Watchman Nee? As he languished in a
Communist prison, his teachings reached out to bless
the worldwide church. John Sung, 'the uncompromising
evangelist', is one of many anointed preachers who
have blazed a trail for God, far beyond the borders of
China. Before the Revolution, Chinese Christians,
without any prompting from the West, formed their
own evangelistic teams and missionary agencies.

The church in China has yet to discover fully her
identity in God, and to realize her calling and destiny.
Is it to be 'the greatest *harvest field*' or the 'greatest *harvest
base*', to help reach a lost and dying world? Shortly
before he died in 1973, Timothy Dzao, 'one of China's
great pastor evangelists', asked Paul Kauffman to
convey this message to the churches of the West:

> I believe that the time has come for the Chinese to preach
> the gospel in the West. This firstly, because we should
> acknowledge our debt to the missionaries who came to
> China with the gospel, and secondly, because God has
> given us Chinese brilliant minds, and a unique ability to
> understand the Scriptures, which were written in an
> Oriental context. I believe that God wants us Chinese to
> bless the West and lead many to Christ.[113]

A prophetic word? If God plans to use this oriental
people to bless the West, might he not first use them to
bless other oriental peoples who are closer to hand?

When Francis Xavier first brought Christianity to
Japan in 1549, he was impressed to see how successfully
the Chinese had brought Confucianism to that nation.
If the Chinese can do that with Confucianism, he
thought, how much more with the Christian gospel?
Believing that China was the key to the evangelism of
Japan, Xavier set sail for China, but he died on an

island off the China coast in 1552. His vision was never fulfilled.

Though Japan had the gospel first, it was China that was the scene of the great missionary movement of the last century. It was China that was destined in this present century to raise up teachers and preachers to touch the outside world. And it is now China, despite the oppressive rule of Marxism, that is now experiencing this great turning to Christ. In preparation for what? Perhaps after 500 years Xavier's vision is destined for a greater fulfilment than even he envisaged.

The cross has always loomed large in the thinking and the experience of the church in China, but never more so than in the last thirty-five years. Engulfed in a river of suffering, they have not quailed before the flood, but, like their master, for the joy set before them, have endured the cross and despised the shame. Is God's time soon to come when he will overthrow every obstacle, satanic and human, and give his servants a worldwide ministry? Is that river of suffering to flow out to a waiting world as a river of blessing?

The last phase of human history prior to Christ's return in glory is to be a time when, according to his own prediction, 'This gospel of the kingdom will be preached in the whole world as a testimony to all nations, and then the end will come.'[114] By the phrase, 'this gospel of the kingdom' Jesus was pinpointing the message as the sign-and-wonder gospel which he and his disciples had preached.[115] Healings and miracles are to characterize that last phase of gospel preaching, just as it characterized the first. Could we find a church anywhere in the world today so ready for such a world-wide task, as is the church in China?

When God finally lifts the Bamboo Curtain and releases these dedicated emissaries of the cross to join hands with Christians of the free world to gather in the final harvest, will they find us ready and willing to pay the price? Not unless there is a significant change in what Chinese Christians who do reach the West are presently finding. One such was Mrs Lee, interviewed by Mrs Marjorie Baker, a former missionary to China. This Chinese lady had been telling of the sufferings that she and her family had endured for thirty years under Communist rule, and then she added:

> I thank God we did not come to Hong Kong in 1948 when we had the opportunity. We might be rich by now in material things, but we would be very poor in spirit. A millionaire could not buy the treasures we now have in Christ.

An old school-friend of mine in Hong Kong, constantly in and out of China, told me how many Chinese Christians are disillusioned by the Christianity they find in the West. It is not so much the prosperity, as the attitude to and pre-occupation with material things. A former missionary said, 'They frequently express a keen disappointment with the shallowness of the church.'

In China the believers know they are engaged in spiritual warfare. They know that they are not fighting a government, a system or an ideology. They are not fighting 'flesh and blood', whether party members, Communist cadres or government officials. They are not fighting lapsed Christians or those believers who have linked themselves with the Three-Self. They are contending against those ruling spirits in the heavenly realms who fight for the kingdom of Satan. But when they reach the West, they find that people do not seem to be aware that there is a war on!

A woman who is a Christian leader in China had

been sharing with her visitors from the West something of the sufferings that she and her husband and family had had to endure for the sake of Christ. When the visitors expressed their sympathy, she replied:

Don't feel sorry for us. At least we are constantly reminded that we are in spiritual warfare. We know for whom we are fighting. We know who are our enemies. And we really *are* fighting. Perhaps we should pray for you Christians outside China. In your leisure, in your affluence, in your freedom, sometimes you no longer realize that you are in a battle.

It is not that the battle in the West is easier than in China. It is just different. In China Satan stalks the land as a roaring lion, seeking whom he may devour. There is no way you can stand as a witness to Christ and avoid meeting him. Either you resist him by faith, and he flees, or you give in to him through fear, and are neutralized. In the West Satan comes as the beguiling serpent. He entices, he lures, he deceives. It all happens before we are even aware that he has infiltrated our ranks. Slowly, almost imperceptibly, our love grows cool. Preoccupation with things replaces passion for Christ. Witness with our lips becomes the exception rather than the rule. 'I'm sure they all know where I stand', becomes our excuse. And because there are so many just like us, no one even whispers the word, 'backslider!' East or West—the temptation may be different, but the answer is the same.

Here then is the message from our brothers and sisters in China:

Embrace the cross and be a conqueror.

Some Chinese Christians, now in the West, are finding that it is in some ways harder to do it here than it was in China. But Scripture assures us that a generation of overcomers will arise who—

> by the blood of the Lamb, and
>
> by the word of their testimony, and
>
> by loving not their lives even unto death—

will finally hurl down Satan from the heavens, and draw forth the triumphant cry, 'Now has come the kingdom.'

NOTES

Chapter 2

1. The modern Pinyin spelling of Chinese names is used throughout, but where the older Wade-Giles system is more familiar to English readers, this has been put in parentheses.
2. Paul Kauffman, *China: The Emerging Challenge*, (Baker Book House 1982) p.127. Reprinted by permission, as are subsequent quotations from this book where only author and page number are indicated in the notes.

Chapter 4

3. Kauffman p.96.   4. Rom 13:1.

Chapter 6

5. Kauffman pp. 170–71.   6. Mt 16:18.

Chapter 7

7. Mt 13:33.   8. Jer 1:10.   9. Dan 11:33.   10. Dan 11:35.
11. Buddhism: with the reopening of Christian churches there has also been a reopening of Buddhist temples, and some resurgence of Buddhism and ancestor worship, but mostly amongst the older people.   12. Fox Butterfield, *China: Alive in the Bitter Sea* (Hodder & Stoughton), reprinted by permission.

Chapter 8

13. Mt 22:21.   14. Rev 21:2; 17:6.   15. Rev 18:4.

Chapter 9

16. Kauffman p.195.   17. Jonathan Chao, Chinese Church Research Centre.

Chapter 10.

18. 'Cadre' is a general term for any worker of the Chinese government or of the Chinese Communist Party. A cadre is roughly equivalent to a civil servant.   19. From *Pray for China*, A Bi-monthly Report (Christian Communications, Hong Kong).   20. Kauffman p.208.   21. From *Pray for China*, A Bi-monthly Report (Christian Communications, Hong Kong).   22. *China and the Church Today* (Chinese Church Research Centre, Hong Kong).   23. Dan 4:35.   24. Job 33:13 (NASB).

Chapter 11

25. Mt 5:11–12.   26. Jn 12:27–28.   27. Acts 5:41.   28. Acts 9:16.   29. Acts 14:22.   30. Phil 1:29.   31. 2 Cor 4:7–12.   32. Acts 20:24.   33. Carl Lawrence, *The Church in China* (Bethany House Publishers, Minneapolis), reprinted by permission.   34. Jonathan Chao, Chinese Church Research Centre.

Chapter 12

35. 1 Thess 1:6–10.   36. 1 Kings 18:38.   37. *China Prayer Letter*, Dec 1983 (Chinese Church Research Centre).   38. 1 Pet 5:10.   39. 2 Cor 4:12.   40. 1 Pet 1:6, 8.   41. 1 Pet 4:1–2.   42. Rev 2:10.   43. Acts 4:10.   44. Acts 5:41–42.   45. Watchman Nee, *The Normal Christian Worker*.   46. David Adeney, *China: Christian Students Face the Revolution* (IVP 1973).   47. Dan 3:18.

Chapter 13

48. David Adeney, *China: Christian Students Face the Revolution* (IVP 1973).   49. 2 Tim 2:3 (TLB).   50. 1 Cor 9:24–27 (RSV). 51. Lk 9:23.   52. 1 Pet 2:11 (RSV).   53. Watchman Nee, *The Normal Christian Worker*.   54. Jn 4:32.   55. Mt 26:41. 56. Watchman Nee, *The Normal Christian Worker*.   57. Phil 4:12.   58. 1 Cor 4:11.   59. 2 Cor 12:7–9.   60. 2 Cor 12:9–10 (italics mine).   61. Heb 11:37.   62. Rev 2:9.   63. Jas 2:5. 64. Heb 10:34.   65. Rom 12:8.   66. Mk 12:43–44.   67. 2 Cor 8:2–4.   68. 1 Tim 6:5, 8.   69. Prov 12:18 (RSV).   70. 1 Pet 4:19.   71. 1 Pet 4:15.   72. 1 Pet 4:16.   73. 1 Pet 4:12–14.   74. 1 Pet 2:19, 21.   75. 1 Pet 3:13–16.   76. 1 Pet 2:23.   77. 2 Cor 4:17.   78. 2 Cor 12:10.

Chapter 14

79. Watchman Nee, *Sit, Walk, Stand* (Victory Press (Kingsway Publications) 1972).   80. Ex 15:11.   81. Jer 29:13.

Chapter 15

82. Kauffman p.229.   83. Carl Lawrence, *The Church in China* (Bethany House Publishers, Minneapolis).   84. Col 2:20–22. 85. Jn 18:36.   86. Mt 6:33.   87. Col 3:1–2 (RSV).   88. 1 Jn 2:15.   89. 1 Jn 2:17.   90. 1 Pet 2:11.   91. Phil 3:20.   92. Gal 6:14.

Chapter 16

93. 1 Cor 12:9–10.   94. Mk 16:18.   95. C. E. Cowman, *Streams in the Desert* (Marshall, Morgan & Scott 1971).

Chapter 17

96. Acts 12:13–15.   97. Kauffman p.199.   98. Kauffman pp.194–5.   99. 1 Cor 14:1.   100. 1 Cor 14:12.   101. 1 Cor 14:5.

Chapter 18

102. 1 Cor 14:26.   103. 1 Cor 12:7.   104. Heb 12:25–29. 105. G. H. Lang, *Church Federation*.

Chapter 19

106. Eph 4:11.   107. From a report in *The Church in China*, Carl Lawrence (Bethany House Publishers, Minneapolis). 108. Heb 13:3.   109. Phil 1:12.   110. *China Prayer Letter*, October 1984 (Chinese Church Research Centre).   111. 1 Tim 2:1–2.   112. Kauffman p.315.

Chapter 20

113. Kauffman p.158.   114. Mt 24:14.   115. Mt 24:23–24; 9:35; 10:7–8.

APPENDIX

For those who wish to be kept up to date with news of what God is doing in China, and of ministries that are reaching the church in that land, the following organizations issue periodical reports, prayer bulletins, magazines etc:

Asian Outreach, GPO Box 3448, Hong Kong.

Chinese Church Research Centre, P.O. Box 312, Shatin Central P.O., N.T., Hong Kong.

China Ministries Department, Christian Communications, P.O. Box 95364, Tsimshatsui, Hong Kong.

Overseas Missionary Fellowship Ltd, China Programme Office, c/o Christchurch, Glebe Road, Bayston Hill, Shrewsbury, SY3 0PZ.

China Prayer Fellowship, Send Barns Lane, Send, Woking, Surrey GU23 7BS.

Open Doors, P.O. Box 47, Ermelo, Holland.

Trans World Radio, 45 London Road, Biggleswade, Bedfordshire SG18 8ED.

Far East Broadcasting Association, 45 High Street, Addlestone, Weybridge, Surrey KT15 1TJ.

Far East Broadcasting Company, P.O. Box 96789, Tsimshatsui, Hong Kong.

Living God's Way
A Course for Discipling New Christians

by Arthur Wallis

We live in a day of exciting growth, when churches are experiencing a new outpouring of the Holy Spirit and new believers are being gathered in.

The challenge is clear. Christians need to be firmly grounded in the truths of Scripture, so that they are equipped to give teaching and pastoral help to new believers.

This course has been specially designed for use in the local church setting, and is ideal for one-to-one discipling. With a clear and straightforward approach it covers the Bible's basic teaching so that the new Christian can gain a thorough understanding of Christian commitment and how it affects every area of life.

Kingsway Publications

The Radical Christian

by Arthur Wallis

God's Holy Spirit is at work to change us into
the likeness of Christ. Do we realize what a
radical change this means?

This book challenges us to re-examine some of
our cherished customs and beliefs. It shows
how Scripture can guide us over such issues as
church unity, water and Spirit baptism, and
denominational loyalty.

The author confesses that this has not been an
easy book to write. Nor will it be easy for us to
receive. It calls for a verdict on God's truth—
and so for a verdict on ourselves. Each one of
us must decide: am I a compromiser, or a
radical?

The axe is laid to the root of the tree.

Kingsway Publications

Pray in the Spirit

by Arthur Wallis

In this book Arthur Wallis concentrates on the ministry of the Holy Spirit in relation to prayer, and investigates the full meaning of the apostle's injunction to 'pray in the Spirit'.

He analyses the spiritual and practical difficulties we encounter, and shows how the Holy Spirit helps us in our weakness and makes up for all our deficiencies. We are encouraged to yield ourselves completely to Him, allowing Him to pray through us.

As we enter into the 'deep things of God' unfolded here we shall discover a new power and effectiveness in our Christian lives.

Kingsway Publications

God's Chosen Fast

by Arthur Wallis

Having proved over many years the great value and blessing of fasting, Arthur Wallis has written this book to share with us what the Bible says about this important and neglected subject. His aim is to deal not only with all the main passages in Scripture that touch on the matter, but also with the practical issues involved.

This is a balanced study which seeks to give to the subject the weight that Scripture gives it and to avoid exaggeration and over-emphasis. The book includes a biblical index, and an appendix dealing with the textual problems surrounding four references to fasting in the New Testament.

k

Kingsway Publications

Into Battle
A manual of the Christian life

by Arthur Wallis

Every person is involved in a spiritual war. Becoming a Christian is to join forces with God against the powers of darkness.

This book is a battle manual of the Christian life. It shows step by step how to enlist and prepare for action, starting with repentance from sin, faith in the saving power of God and then baptism in water and in the Holy Spirit.

But it does not stop there. The book goes on to show how victory over the enemy can become an increasing reality in every part of our lives.

Kingsway Publications